LEAVING
INDONESIA

Sister Mary Lou,

LEAVING INDONESIA

Thanks for the support!

Kevin Lee

April 4, 2017

Kevin Lee

Names have been changed and non-historical time sequences adjusted. In all other regards, this is a work of non-fiction.
Category: Travel Writing / Asia / Southeast

© 2016 Kevin Lee
Published by Kevin Lee
8 Herbert Pl.
Yonkers, NY 10704

Design, layout and photo editing by Bryan Close, The Light Dynamic.
Cover Photos by Kevin Lee.
Map on top of page x credited to The Australia National University – College of Asia and the Pacific.
Map on bottom of page x created using MapHub.
All interior photos by Kevin Lee except photo on bottom of page 174 credited to Desmon Nusantara.
Author photo by Erlangga.

ISBN-13: 978-1535543262
ISBN-10: 1535543264

for everyone at
Padang's *Pasar Seni*

for **Desmon**

CONTENTS

Indonesia's Timeline

1603 – Dutch arrive in the Indies.

1942 – Japanese kick the Dutch out.

1945 – Sukarno declares Indonesia's independence two days after WWII ends: Declares that all land that fell under Dutch Rule, as well as Portuguese East Timor, is considered Indonesia.

1945 – Dutch with help from the British try to recapture Indo.

1949 – Dutch forces surrender and leave Indo.

1953 – Aceh's first rebellion against Indo Rule.

1958 – West Sumatra and Ambon's first rebellion against Indo Rule.

1965 – A complex coup pushes Sukarno out of power and paves the way for Suharto to become Indo's second president.

1965 – Pramoedya Ananta Toer, Indo writer, is arrested and spends the next 14 years in prison.

1969 – A controversial vote legitimizes Papua's inclusion into Indo.

1980 – *This Earth of Mankind,* the first book of Pramoedya's Buru Quartet, is published.

1998 – A revolution removes Suharto from power.

1999 – Chaos ensues over many parts of Indo including Ambon, where a 3-year civil war breaks out between Muslims and Christians.

1999 – East Timor becomes only region to break away from Indo Rule and gain independence.

2002 – A nightclub in Bali is bombed by an Al-Qaeda linked terrorist organization.

2004 – Boxing Day Tsunami strikes Aceh.

2008 – Kevin Lee arrives on first trip to Indo.

2009 – Kevin Lee spends two months in Indo, mainly in Ambon, looking for work.

2010 – Kevin Lee works as a visiting professor at Andalas University in Padang, West Sumatra.

2011 – Kevin Lee travels across Indo from Aceh to Papua, a trip this book is based on.

Indonesia Maps

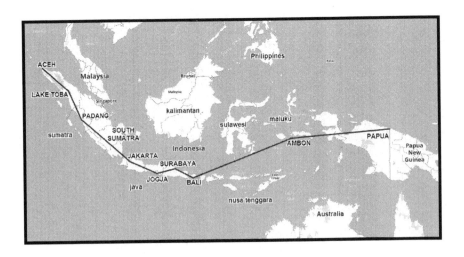

"What can I say about the world? We hardly know anything about the world here, and the world knows nothing about Indonesia."

-Pramoedya Ananta Toer [1]

LEAVING

INDONESIA

Introduction

I was somewhere between Lake Toba and Siantar, North Sumatra when the drugs started to take hold.

Scratch that.

~~I was somewhere between Lake Toba and Siantar, North Sumatra when the drugs started to take hold.~~

There were no drugs. Possession of drugs is punishable by death in Indonesia, it says so right on the visa in my hand that expires tomorrow. Besides, I forget things so often and incessantly daydream, and struggle to put two thoughts together on paper or in speech. Drugs were not going to help. No, I was on Day 29 of my great Indonesian adventure when it finally hit me. My head was trapped in writing a worthless book that still did not even have an intro.

I had set out to write the Great Indonesian Travel Story. I was tired of seeing bookshelves overflowing with titles on China, Japan, and India. Who was writing about the country that was a continent in itself? Over 300 ethnic groups speaking hundreds of different languages, mixing, sharing customs, warring as one, warring on each other; this is the land that gets rocked almost weekly by a new natural disaster, the society spectrum that includes care-free surfers and radical Islamists; the country where Barack Obama spent a chunk of his childhood and drifters like me sought a life in the world's last frontiers yet to be conquered by KFC and Starbucks. This book was going to take all the dramatic history, current events and social issues of this 17,000 plus island archipelago and tell it through the raw lens of my seven month journey from the western shores of Sumatra to the jungles of Papua.

Whenever someone asked what the book was going to be about, I would tell them it was not going to be a personal diary or a travel guide or an overly academic study. I knew exactly what the book would not be.

The book would paint a picture of Indonesia in 2011, how it was born and the direction it is headed in. The story would grow from conversations with the country's people; how they saw themselves and the world, what they wanted out of life and what obstacles and opportunities stood in front of them. The book would be a mosaic (pause for dramatic effect), small glimpses into a few of the hundreds of ethnic groups, remarkably distinct from one another, yet fusing together to illuminate what less than a century ago was only an idea – Indonesia.

The book would capture the temper and the time of one country through the eyes of one backpacking, knowledge-thirsty, young man. It would one day take its place with the dynamic works of other times like Jack Kerouac's *On the Road*, the book that set off generations of wanderers, dreamers and truth seekers on journeys to experience for the sake of experience.

The tale that conceived in me my first real connection to a writer and freed others writers from literary constraints, proving that for some, stream of conscious writing was the only chance you had of an ounce truth coming out of you.

My book would be heralded around the world. Various Indonesian ethnic groups would thank me for getting their story out as well as tripling tourism in their towns. World leaders would have a captivating guidebook to help them understand the fourth most populated country on earth. Loads of Americans would run out and get a passport, not only to visit Indonesia, but all the far off places their hearts always desired to see. Muslim-Christian relations would improve. Back in my hometown, New Yorkers would stop protesting the "Ground Zero Mosque" due to Islamophobia, and continue to protest once they learned that their sleep would be interrupted by ear-piercing Arabic at 5:00 AM every morning.

***

So what had gone wrong? I had started my trip by splitting one month in two of the most fascinating places on earth: Aceh and Toba.

Aceh is ground zero to the worst natural disaster on record this century – an earthquake and tsunami that wiped out 170,000 people and most of the capital city, Banda Aceh, that had once stood as a powerful nation state, trading its pepper and gold all over the world and hosting extravagant parties for neighboring kings where VIPs would arrive atop elephants. And if Indonesia truly is a battleground of freewheeling Western ideals versus more conservative Islamic values, Aceh is the Islamic corner of the ring. Sharia law, the rule of the land, caning the appropriate punishment for adultery and movie theaters banned because of the imminent threat of what couples might do. (Imagine how it infuriates the government that the best Indonesian pornos are covertly filmed here.) This is a land that fought as hard as any place on earth against all aggressors from the Netherlands to Jakarta. It took a 60-foot wave to finally pause the war on Boxing Day, 2004. On a walk around Banda Aceh's well frequented coffee shops you will find stone-faced, unemployed rebel soldiers as well as young entrepreneurs making a fortune selling trips to Mecca. You have to love any religion that stands on five pillars, one being a road trip.

And then there was Lake Toba, Southeast Asia's largest lake, formed 74,000 years ago by the most powerful volcanic eruption of the last two million years. So devastating it covered South Asia with ash, blocked out the sun, lowered world temperatures by 60 degrees and threw us into an Ice Age, while also managing to wipe out most life on Earth. Today Samosir Island, just slightly larger than Chicago, is actually the caldera of that deadly volcano reemerged from Lake Toba and a pristine home to about a thousand people including many farmers and woodcarvers. I guess that's how it is. One day you are dictating what temperature the world is, and the next day, or 74,000 years later, you have to read my book to know where it is.

If the ancient history is not enough of a draw to Toba, the Bataks, its inhabitants are. In the early 1900s American travel writer Alexander Powell described how a branch of Bataks handled their elderly, claiming that "when their relatives become too old and infirm to be of further use. . . The aged victim climbs a lemon-tree, beneath which his relatives stand in a circle, wailing the deathsong, the weird, monotonous chant being continued until the condemned one summons the courage to throw himself to the ground, whereupon the members of his family promptly dispatch him with clubs, cut up his body, roast the meat, and eat it." Every Batak I have read this to has been highly insulted and vehemently discredits the truth of this account, even though it is clearly stated in a free book on my iPad.

So after twenty-nine days on the road, many hours spent in front of computer screens, months of planning, or at least talking about planning and dozens of promises by people to buy my book, this was what I had to show for it – three paragraphs. Maybe I could lower my expectations a bit and just write one paragraph on each of the places I found interesting. A mini-history/ guide book of Indonesia. I could put in lots of photographs and little drawings to fill up the pages and make my friends and family feel better about paying $15 for it. I would need to find someone to draw the pictures for me.

What was I missing? I was envisioning the book as a raw creation that broke the rules of travel writing as I sat in coffee shops trying not to let anyone see I was reading *Lonely Planet's Guide to Travel Writing*. I needed some chance occurrence, a dashing Brazilian to knock me off my bike or a mobster to give me a job at a cabstand parking cars or shining shoes.

Maybe I needed a sidekick. Charlie Babbitt had his autistic brother. Che Guevara shared a motorcycle with his womanizing friend. John Steinbeck had his French Poodle, Charlie, sitting shotgun. I bet if I had a French Poodle with me this trip would get a lot more exciting.

Twenty-nine days into my epic journey, I was somewhere between Lake Toba and Siantar, North Sumatra with no confidence in my writing, no drugs, no more days left on my visa, no French Poodle and no story. But maybe there was still hope. After all, even *On the Road* began with a pointless trip to Bear Mountain in the rain.

Kantor Imigrasi
Siantar, North Sumatra

"Indonesian bureaucracy exists to see that procedures are followed. Government officials see themselves as in positions of authority and expect to be treated with respect."

-Customs and Etiquette of Indonesia[2]

As I step off the bus in Siantar, there is one thing that is clear to me. I need to start from scratch. Forget the plan. Start with the basics. I recall a piece of advice a teacher once gave me, "When you are trying to figure out what you want to do with your life, just ask yourself three questions. 1) What do you love to do? 2) What are you good at? And 3) what does the world need?" The third question is out of my league and the second question depresses me. I concentrate on the first. Actually, I simplify it a bit. "What do I really want to do right now?"

We are standing at the bus stop and Charlie, my little Batak friend, is staring at me as if I am going to slip into a permanent catatonic state. We are on our way to the Siantar *Kantor Imigrasi* (Immigration Office). Charlie has offered to be my sponsor in case I run into any problems, which if you are a foreigner in an Indonesian immigration office is almost guaranteed.

What do I want to do? Do I even want to stay in Indonesia?

I have more than six months until I am due back home in New York. I have about a million Indonesian rupiah in my backpack (don't get excited, approximately US $100), $3,232 in my checking account, $11 in my savings account and a friend who owes me a few hundred bucks. Where am I going to go, Paris? Even if I wanted to go to Africa or South America the airfare and initial weeks of trying to gain my footing would break me. There are other parts of Asia, but I had been all around Asia when I was living the good life as an international school teacher in China. I had made up my mind then that Indonesia had the largest number of superlatives of any place I had been. The most stunning landscapes, warmest people, fascinating history and extremely important for me, the easiest language, which I have already made some headway into. I have to stay in Indonesia. Leaving would be like running out on a true love just because I don't know what to buy her for her birthday.

So I decide we will continue with the mission for today, attempt to renew my visa for another thirty days and figure out the rest later. Two guys in their early-20s pull up on motorbikes. Charlie had called them while I was dazed out in my quarter life crisis. Charlie introduces one of them to me as his cousin. This is always a confusing part of Indonesia. If you are like me and for whatever reason need to know if someone is a biological relative or just an acquaintance close enough to deserve the title, getting to the bottom of it can drive you mad.

"Your cousin?"

"Yes."

"Real cousin?"

"Yes."

"Like actually family, blood cousin?"

"Yes, like that."

"Like one of your parents and one of his parents are brothers and sisters?"

"Yes."

"Like one of your parents and one of his parents grew up in the same house or came from the same womb?"

"Oh no, not that kind of cousin."

I hop on the back of a motorbike with Charlie's "cousin" who was kind enough to grab a friend in between his classes and give us a lift to the immigration office. We pull up to a cream colored government building. Charlie rolls down his polyester pants before we go in.

Entering an Indonesian immigration office feels a lot like entering a confession booth, only you have no idea what you did wrong. You need to be extremely respectful, almost to the point of looking defeated. You can show no arrogance. Do not even smile when the woman with the patch on her shoulder says, *"Ahhhh Amerika."* Do not in any way give off an air that you expect your visa to be renewed. I always try to make it seem like I have just dropped in to pay my respects. I carry myself with an attitude that says, "I was wondering if it is not any trouble, if it just might cross your mind to consider extending my visa, even for just a few more days. Because this is such a wonderful country kept strong by its hard working government employees, and I would be delighted, grateful and honored to spend just a little more time here."

Another useful word to say as frequently as possible is *Bu*, Indonesian for mother, but used as a sign of respect toward any older woman. When you need something, it is impossible to use the word *Bu* enough. Charlie and I walk into the almost empty lobby and step up to the counter. My bag of *Bu's* is ready to go.

"Ya Bu, Saya suka Indonesia sekali, Bu." (Yes *Bu*, I really like Indonesia, *Bu*.)

"Ya Bu, Aku dari America, Bu." (Yes *Bu*, I am from America, *Bu*.)

"Ya Bu, Saya mau hari lagi di visaku, Bu." (Yes *Bu*, I would like to extend my visa, *Bu*.)

"Ma'af Bu, saya tidak ingat apa pertanyaan mereka bertanya di Konsulat Indonesia di Kota New York, Bu." (Sorry *Bu*, I do not remember what questions I was asked at the Indonesian consulate in New York, *Bu*.)

"Tidak Bu, Saya tidak orang Cina, Bu." (No *Bu*, I am not Chinese, *Bu*.)

"Saya tahu namaku Lee, Bu. Itu nama yang luar biasa juga, Bu." (I know my last name is Lee, *Bu*. It is a rare Irish name too, *Bu*.)

"Kakek dan Nanek Saya dari Irlandia, Bu." (My grandparents were from Ireland, *Bu*.)

"Ya Bu, Saya tahu saya bukan orang Cina." (Yes *Bu*, I am sure that I am not Chinese.)

She walks back to her desk, and I stand behind the counter staring at my shoes. *Bu* is counting the days on the calendar with her finger to see when my visa expires. All of March, now on to April, her finger finally stopping on tomorrow's square. She walks back with my passport in her hand. I am expecting to be lectured on why I waited so long to renew my visa and that it is extremely unreasonable to expect this office to get around to putting a stamp on it by tomorrow, especially with the Chinese name and all. Instead she points to the sponsorship on my visa, Andalas University. She wants to know what my connection is to this well respected university in West Sumatra, the oldest Indonesian university outside of Java. I am prepared for this inquiry, and I launch into a long diatribe in almost fluent Indonesian. I will recall it only in its English translation.

"I worked at Andalas for two semesters, *Bu*. I taught English in the Faculty of Economics. I began teaching in January of 2010 and worked through the end of the year. Andalas has invited me back to learn more about Indonesia and to support me in whatever ways they can in writing this book. Maybe they will even publish it themselves. Actually, I have a letter from a member the Economics Department right here, inviting me to work with her on creating a debate club. And when I pass through Padang in a couple weeks (this is where I start looking up and to the right to access the creative part of my brain since a half hour ago I was considering moving to Uganda), I will meet with her to get this program off the ground to benefit any and all students eager to improve their English....*Bu*."

I find it hard to contain my pride, I was rolling my "r"s like a champ, and I feel like a man ready to get thirty more days stamped on that visa. Still I control myself and patiently await *Bu*'s response.

Bu reaffirms that Andalas was my sponsor when I entered Indonesia. I follow a few sentences, but eventually lose her, and I am forced to wait for Charlie to relay the translation. Charlie looks worried. He turns to me after saying a round of *Bu*'s.

"Kevin, she can't renew your visa here if you are still associated with Andalas. If you have no connection with the university, then I can be your sponsor and she can give you a new visa that will give you 30 more days to stay in the country."

Ahhh, it's time to tell the same story, but this time highlight all different aspects. Charlie and *Bu* wait for me to gather my thoughts in Indonesian.

16

"You see, *Bu*, I did work at Andalas, but that was way back in 2010. I am not receiving any salary from the university right now, and I am actually a little disappointed with the level of support I have received from them in regard to this book. Yes, someone at Andalas wrote a letter to help me get this visa, but as you can see that visa expires tomorrow, cutting my official ties to the university forever. And actually, that renewal letter I showed you before was not even from a faculty member, just a lowly student."

Bu starts pulling out the paperwork for my sponsorship and new visa. Charlie and I nod at each other as if we have just been through the trenches together. After sending me outside a few times to pay for copies of various forms, Charlie and I start filling out the paperwork. We fill out forms, trading papers every few seconds, "I need your signature here." "You sign this one under my signature." By the end of all the form signing I am convinced I have just entered a common law marriage with my little Batak friend.

Charlie tells me that we must give *Bu* a tip. In a country where tipping is not even customary at restaurants, a tip is a polite way of saying bribe. The last form I must buy from *Bu* costs 10,000 rupiah ($1). I hand *Bu* a 50,000 rupiah ($5) bill. She smiles and says she does not have any small money to give me. I smile back. *Bu* has her tip, and I have a date with *Bu* tomorrow afternoon to pick up my new visa.

Makasih Bu! (Thanks *Bu!*)

1

Padang, West Sumatra

With approximately 200 million speakers, the Indonesian/Malaysian language, also known as *Bahasa* (Language), is tied with Portuguese as the eighth most spoken language in the world. *Bahasa* Indonesia and *Bahasa* Malay, spoken in neighboring Malaysia, are similar enough to be grouped as one language. Of the fifteen most spoken languages, *Bahasa* is by far the easiest for your average native English speaker to learn. If you do not want to learn a language that looks like this 雞,

this ভেড়া ,

this 虎,

this свинья,

this مگرمچھ

this台州

this ม้าลาย

this حصان

or this كَح

you can eliminate two thirds of that Top 15 list. Actually, just copying and pasting some of those words into a document creates a stubborn, grey background and causes your keyboard to start typing backwards. Who needs that? With the remaining European languages you have to deal with tenses, choosing the correct gender for a word, conjugating verbs, plus the fact that Europeans hate it when you mangle their language.

The *Bahasa* language includes none of the hassles above. It uses Roman letters and is almost 100% phonetic. It shares many cognate words with the English language such as *taksi* (taxi), *unik* (unique), *erobik* (aerobic), *komedi* (comedy), *es krim* (ice cream), *doktor* (doctor), *komputer* (computer), *wiski* (whisky). A glance at the spelling of certain words in *Bahasa* Indonesia will make you think that a kindergartener sounded out each word and gave it his best shot.

Bahasa also possesses a beautiful simplicity in forming more complex words from simpler words. Room is *rumah*. Food is *makan*. Restaurant is *rumah makan*. *Sakit* means pain. *Rumah Sakit* means hospital. *Luar* means outside. *Keluar* is Exit (Literally: go outside). *Biasa* means usual. *Luar biasa*, Unusual (literally: outside usual). To show tense you never need to change a word by adding *ed* or *ing*.   Just add a time marker such as *besok* (tomorrow) or *satu minggu lalu* (one week ago).   To pluralize a word all you have to do is say it twice. If you want more than one banana just say, *Saya mau pisang-pisang*.   And Indonesians have no pretentiousness toward their language. Any attempt at speaking *Bahasa* Indonesian will be met with smiles and encouragement, and all too often an overly enthusiastic teacher who points at everything in sight and tells you its Indonesian name.

Surprisingly, this Indonesian language is not the native tongue of the vast majority of the archipelago. The island of Java, which accounts for one half (120 million) of Indonesia's population, has a completely different language, Javanese (the 16th most spoken language on earth). Even in the early 20th Century few inhabitants of the Dutch East Indies could actually speak what would be proclaimed Indonesia's national language in 1945.

Prior to the 1920s, history seems to judge much of the occupied East Indies as a place where people were uneducated, servile to their Dutch masters and even unquestioning of the authority over them, as if freedom was not even imagined, much less contemplated. The Dutch had built railroads and schools, introduced vaccinations and a level of order.   For Dutch colonialists, these improvements eased their moral consciences while also making the job of strengthening the royal Dutch monarchy easier, while pillaging these islands of its natural resources, most notably coffee, tea, tobacco, rubber, sugar, nutmeg, cloves and cinnamon.

For centuries prior to the arrival of colonialists, and to some extent still in some areas today, the islands of Indonesia had been a land of kingdoms. This form of government instilled into its people an unquestioning respect for power and an emphasis on knowing your place in society. Both elements played a pivotal role establishing and upholding Dutch control in the Indies. The Dutch bought off *rajahs* (kings) to legitimize their authority. *Rajahs* passed orders down that were carried out by native government officials. In later colonial years people of mixed blood were often appointed to the highest positions of authority. But no matter who was relaying the orders, the best interests of the Netherlands were always kept.

Pramoedya Ananta Toer, Indonesia's most internationally recognized writer, used the characters in his epic four volume work, the Buru Quartet, to portray the evolution of thinking in the Indies. In one passage, Pram's protagonist, Minke, listens to his mother, whom he respects and loves deeply, scold him for wanting too much out of life. The words of Minke's mother epitomize native thinking in the colonial-Indies, "To free men from the burdens made by other men. . . That is not Javanese. A Javanese does something with no other motive than to do it. Orders come from Allah, from the gods, from the *Raja*. After a Javanese has carried out the order, he will feel satisfied because he has become himself. And then he awaits the next order."[3]

Minke bows humbly, holding his response in his heart for the time being, "She was a Javanese woman and she had her own wisdom. And I would never be able to marry a woman like her. Forgive me, mother. I am travelling another path."[4]

With the beginning of the 20th Century many young people of the Indies began clearing their own path. In 1928 political activists at a youth congress in Batavia (Jakarta's name as a Dutch colony) announced "a Pledge of the Youth" to achieve liberation from colonialism. "One nation with one language, Indonesian; and one homeland Indonesia." A bold statement considering not only the power and control of the Dutch empire, but also because of the fact that the people of these islands never considered itself one country, just a string of islands currently ruled by foreign white-skinned, blue-eyed rulers. And most people from Aceh to Papua had no idea what the "Indonesian language" meant.

The Dutch were able to stave off colonial rebellions longer than their European neighbors by limiting education and blocking information from reaching the Indies. Very few Natives of the Indies were offered more than the most basic education. Even the few Natives who attained higher education would have been taught by Dutch instructors, not the people most likely to speak about the rise of Asian powers, such as the Philippines' declaration of independence from Spain in 1898 or Japan's victory over Russia in 1904.

In the 1920s an Indonesian intellectual and nationalistic enlightenment budded into existence. Democratic, Communist and Capitalist ideas began mixing with the teachings of Islam and the seeds of a revolution were formed. By the time Indonesia declared her Independence on August 17, 1945 those seeds had flourished.

***

Read any travel guide on Padang, the capital of West Sumatra and you will find descriptions such as "crowded, polluted, humid, a transit stop for the Mentawai Islands and Bukittinggi (*bukit*: hill, *tinggi*: tall), "The Town in the Tall Hills." The majority of tourists passing through are surfers on their way to Mentawai to check out the islands that are continually ranked one of the top five places in the world for surfing. Most of these surfers get one night of drinking on *Jalan* (Street) Hyuk Warum and then flee Padang by way of a chartered speed boat.

I stayed in Padang a little longer. While trying to decide, which part of Indonesia I wanted to live in, I wandered on to the campus of Andalas University. A tall undergrad, wearing a *jilbab* (headscarf) approached me and asked if she could help. I told her I was considering living in Padang and wanted to know if there might be a teaching opportunity. She introduced me to a young professor, also wearing a *jilbab*, who was a former Miss West Sumatra. Former Miss West Sumatra informed me that she was scheduled to teach a business writing class in five minutes, and asked if I would like to teach the class for her. I brainstormed some ideas, reminded myself to speak slowly and clearly and managed to teach a one-hour class to about 20 undergraduates. The next morning Miss West Sumatra introduced me to the dean of the faculty of economics, who resembled Ho Chi Minh. He offered me a position as a visiting professor for $300/month and a free dorm room. I asked for $1,000/month and a free dorm room. We settled on $300/month and a free dorm room, and Padang became my home in Indonesia.

Andalas University is located in the hills, looking down on a city of one million, and out toward the Indian Ocean. I would usually finish work in the middle of the afternoon heat and head straight to one of the *warungs* (small open-air restaurants) along *Pantai* (beach) Padang to enjoy one of my favorite Indonesian dishes. *Rujuk*, a popular beach food around the country is a mix of, pineapple, mango, apple, papaya and any other tropical fruit on hand covered in a dark, spicy peanut sauce. *Kopi susu* (milk coffee) is a drink that I probably acquired a clinical addiction to. *Susu* literally means milk, but usually refers to condensed milk, a substance not very different from cake icing that when mixed with Sumatra's home grown coffee produces a sweet, potent drink. Indonesians do not use typical coffee machines so *kopi susu* is served in a six ounce glass, two ounces of white *susu* on the bottom and four ounces of black unfiltered *kopi* on top. One must give ample time to let the thin coffee grains settle to the bottom and remember not to swallow them on your last gulp.

In 2010, I spent at least two hundred evenings along Padang's coast sipping *kopi susu*, reading books about Indonesia or by Indonesian authors and watching the sun dip into the Indian Ocean triggering some of the most dramatic sunsets in the world. Some evenings I felt more adventurous and set out to explore more of Padang. I was greeted by teenage boys blasting Indonesian pop music from their parents' cars and a chorus of *"Bule! Bule!"* (white person). A wrong turn would land me in Padang's market filled with toys, fruit, t-shirts, pirated DVDs, random fluorescent objects, standstill traffic even if you're on foot and a whole lot of shouting. The sidewalk that connects *Jalan* Hyuk Warum to the *pasar* (market) is filled with death traps. Rectangular holes, large enough to fit your 1980s television, that drop straight down three to six feet into garbage and sewage. With no street lights to be found, I was amazed that Padang did not lead the world in missing tourists.

One evening I made it through the teenagers and pop music, around the death traps and avoided the *pasar* to find one of the finest hidden gems in all of Indonesia. *Pasar Seni* (art colony) is a strip of one-room art galleries adjoined to bamboo terraces where painters, musicians, wood carvers and dancers hang out drinking *kopi* and smoking cigarettes.

Locals of all ages drop in frequently to chat with the men and women who create the art that fills *Pasar Seni*. To refer to this place as a market is a bit deceiving. For a foreigner, walking through a market in Southeast Asia can be a psychedelic trip filled with vendors grabbing at you and often coaxing you into bargaining. At *Pasar Seni*, almost any piece of art can be bought. But for these artists, selling seems to be an afterthought.

Mamat, a young artist originally from a nearby town called *Sulit Air* (Difficult to Find Water), specializes in West Sumatran landscapes and a unique type of art that involves humans whose skin resembles the interior of a tree, as if their age could be counted by the rings on their body. While living in Padang, I watched Mamat spend almost a year on one painting. Although when asked, he was clueless as to when he began a particular piece of work. *Da* (title for a slightly older Minang man) Jon, a local with dreadlocks, personifies nature in many of his pieces with water, land and sky combining to create faces that appear to be crying out. Much of the paintings and wood carvings in *Da* Jon's shop were created in the wake of Padang's September 30, 2009 earthquake, which killed many of his friends.

As I stroll through these quiet rooms, admiring their work, not a single artist pressures me to buy a piece of art. When I inquire about prices, I learn from their befuddled faces that they have not contemplated the monetary value of their work. I once heard an art critic comment on how many great artists who learn how to market themselves and profit financially from their art make their way to Bali and Jogja. But the ones who never bother to learn the game, who never bother to take a second of time away from their art, will always fill places like Padang's *Pasar Seni.*

Many of the painters and their friends are talented musicians. During the day, you may hear a guitar being strummed in one room or the beating of a drum from another. At night these sounds come together. Some nights the music holds a certain melody that seamlessly merges with sounds of the breaking and rebirth of each nearby wave. If you want to learn an instrument, there is surely someone to teach you. During my time in Padang, foreign students studying at Andalas University would join in some nights, bringing their own sounds from Madagascar, Canada, India, Mexico and the Ivory Coast.

Desmon, the only regular at *Pasar Seni* that speaks fluent English, can be found most nights singing and playing a guitar. He was still a teenager when he began suffering severe chest pains. He says singing is the only thing that makes the pain go away. He knows hundreds of '80s and '90s rock songs by heart, from U2 to Nine Inch Nails, Pearl Jam, Sonic Youth, Guns n' Roses, Oasis and the Cure. But anyone who has ever sat with Desmon for a jam session knows that as the night wears on, Bob Marley's words are the only ones coming from Desmon's mouth.

Many of my most memorable nights in Indonesia were spent listening to the music of *Pasar Seni* while drinking rum mixed with *teh botol* (a brand of iced tea) from a plastic bag and straw. Everyone contributes to the sound whether they are singing, playing a guitar or violin, beating drums or tapping a fork against an empty beer bottle.

Most of the regulars at *Pasar Seni* are single men from teens to early 30s. A few of the more established artists live at *Pasar Seni*, simply laying down a mat in the middle of their shop to sleep on at night. *Da* Jon shares his art shop with his wife and two children. Most of the guys live in a nearby art community called Belanak, a one story house with walls covered in artwork and floors lined with sleeping mats. While staying in Padang on this trip across the country, I had my own mat at Belanak to sleep on. In the mornings I would go to the well to fetch water for my shower, hurling a bucket with an adjacent rope down about fifteen feet and then filling up a tall barrel. Then once in the bathroom, bucketing the water again from the barrel to dump over me. The water, which is a little colder than room temperature, always feels good after waking up sweaty with mosquitoes buzzing in my ear all night, undeterred by the anti-*nyamuk* (mosquito) spray I am doused with or the anti-*nyamuk* coils that burn all night a couple feet from my mat.

The men at Belanak have a genuine interest in the world, in how other people see it and live in it. They were far more inquiring about the politics, customs and perceptions of the outside world than most college professors I met. Everyone at Belanak gives to the community what they can, money earned from selling a piece of artwork, playing music at restaurants or some other odd job like painting a city wall. Not everyone gives an equal share, but this does not seem to be a problem. Usually twice a day whoever has money will drive a motorbike to a local *warung* and buy a hefty portion of white rice with a side of fish, chicken or beef dipped in a local sauce. When that person returns to the house he will lay out a long green leaf in the middle of the front room and dump the rice, meat and sauce on top of it. Whoever is home will circle around taking fistfuls of *makan* (food) with their right hands (Left hands are used in place of toilet paper and for nothing else) and stuffing their faces, as plenty of rice falls back down on the leaf. Although I might be regarded as thin in America, the guys at Belanak consider me fat, or at least needing a lot of food. While they seem to be a bit aggressive with each other when it comes to snatching up all the small pieces of fish, chicken or beef, when my section of leaf is left with only rice, someone always nonchalantly and without making eye contact flings a piece of meat in my direction.

The guys always eat in silence. Meals are a time to enjoy the food in front of you. There is no need to spoil it with words. The stray cats, which wander in and out of the windows of Belanak, try to slice through our circle. Erlunga, who seems to be Belanak's caretaker, is the only one the cats listen to when he tells them to knock it off. Sometimes a cat comes into my room with a roach in her mouth, only to let it go for split seconds at a time as she catches it just before it reaches my mat, giving me a deeper understanding of the phrase, "Look what the cat dragged in." Erlunga always saves a few scraps for the cats.

Just one day inside of *Belanak* gave me a better understanding of how communally people are capable of living. While not all Indonesians live like this, a communal sense of living is engrained in the mindset of the country. While the cities may see increases in their inhabitants year after year, the village mentality is showing no signs of fading. Neighbors see the task of disciplining your child as being as much their job as it is yours. Staying abreast of the latest gossip and personal matters of each household in your neighborhood is a staple of Indonesian society. In Surabaya, East Java I would learn that some neighborhoods actually set up checkpoints to ensure that single college students are not getting any ideas of cohabiting for a night. The will to surrender individuality and the inherent acceptance of communal living make it easy to see why communism, at least in theory, was so appealing for millions in the early years of Indonesia. In the early 1960s Indonesia was home to the largest communist party in the world outside of China.

***

Relative to its population, the Minangkabau or Minang people of West Sumatra contributed more than their fair share of revolutionary leaders not only to defeat the Dutch, but to lay the foundation of what an Indonesian government and nation would look like. In cities all across Indonesia today, the Minang names of Mohammad Hatta (First Vice-President), Sutan Syahir (First Prime Minister) and Tan Malaka (an early, influential political thinker) decorate street signs.

The Minang people, who even today make up just 3% of Indonesia's population, possess a cultural tradition called *merantau* that has provided them with an edge on the hundreds of other ethnic groups. It is expected by family and society that a Minang man at some point in his younger years leave his home far behind to create a better life for himself. Single Minang women are not encouraged to take part, but when couples marry young, *merantau* naturally becomes a shared experience. The endeavor may be educational or entrepreneurial. Although many eventually return to their homeland, this is not a requirement. The most important element of *merantau* is that one leaves, which is the literal definition of the word.*

At *Pasar Seni,* Mamat is performing his *merantau,* having left his hometown deep in the mountains to come to Padang. *Da* Jon went to Jogja, Central Java to

---

* Instead of *Leaving Indonesia,* the Indonesian title of this book (when it is published in Indonesian) is *Merantau Orang Amerika* (An American's *Merantau*).

study art for his. Many other artists who are originally from Padang are preparing for their own *merantau*.

The practice of *merantau* has led the Minang people to learn from other ethnic groups of the archipelago and to leave their mark on other islands. One of the reasons Indonesians chose the language they did, which was native only to parts of Sumatra, is because the language of Minang merchants was already being taken up in ports and shipping towns as the language of trade. You can not travel to any corner of Indonesia without finding a *Rumah Makan Minang* (Minang Restaurant) or a *Rumah Makan Padang* (Padang Restaurant). In fact, in most towns Minang owned restaurants out number local ones.

However much the Minang people contributed in the early years to the creation of Indonesia, the country's first president would be a man from Java. That man's vision of what Indonesia would be would decide the fate of the country's first twenty years. His ego and the circumstances that allowed his coup on September 30, 1965 would decide Indonesia's fate until almost the end of the 20th Century.

***

Whether one had warm or cold feelings for Indonesia's first president, many would agree that Sukarno was a larger than life figure. He spoke with varying proficiency: German, French, Dutch, English, Japanese, Arabic, Javanese, Sudanese, Balinese and Indonesian. When the Soviets started demanding too much from this Southeast Asian leader with one name, he leaned closer to the US. When the US accused the little guy in the Muslim cap of being too socialist he drifted back toward Russia, accepting hundreds of millions of dollars in aid from each country while constantly enraging both. In 1955 he hosted the Asia-Africa Conference, which would eventually give birth to the Non-Aligned Movement, a group of states that are not formally aligned with or against any major power bloc.* The conference, held in Bandung, brought together the heads of twenty-nine states, mostly former colonies. It was held on the principle that the US and the Soviet Union are two big babies that want to fight and want the rest of the world to take a side, therefore dividing us apart. So let them fight and concern ourselves with the development of our own countries.

Sukarno, the son of a poor Javanese school teacher and a Balinese mother, survived a series of illnesses as a boy. He attended secondary school in Surabaya and lived at that time with a prominent civic and religious figure who treated him as a foster son and financed his education. He was one of the first dozen Indonesians accepted to a new Dutch technical college in Bandung, where he earned a degree in civil engineering. There he befriended a Minang man,

---

* Over a half century later the Non Aligned Movement still acts as a thorn in U.S. foreign policy. In August 2012 the leaders of 120 state countries met in Tehran to unanimously decree support for Iran's pursuit of nuclear energy while criticizing the American-led attempt to punish Iran with economic sanctions.

Muhammad Hatta, who would eventually become his, and the nation's first vice-president,

Sukarno became known for his superb oratory skills and his bold vision for Indonesia. In 1929, at the age of 28, that vision and those skills would land Sukarno in a Dutch colonial prison. He spent the majority of the next thirteen years of his life in exile, reading and conversing with other political dissidents. In 1942 when Japan's military forces arrived and the Dutch fled, abandoning the land they had colonized for over 350 years without firing a shot, Sukarno was reunited with Hatta. Together they collaborated with the Japanese through the end of World War II.

On August 15, 1945 Japan surrendered to the Allied Forces. With the Japanese occupying forces in disarray and the Allied Forces yet to arrive, their time had come. Thanks to Sukarno, his Minang friends Dr. Hatta and Sutan Sjahrir, and thousands of other revolutionaries, Indonesia was prepared to be born.

As Sukarno hesitated to declare independence, his followers did not wait around for their predestined leader to gather his thoughts. In the pre-dawn hours of August 16th, Sukarno was kidnapped by three members of a revolutionary youth group, moved to a secret location and lectured at gunpoint on the need to declare independence immediately.

Sukarno later reflected on the incident, "The funniest thing that ever happened to me. There was I, flanked on all sides by angry young men brandishing guns and threatening me. I could have put them over my knee and spanked them, for I knew most of them from childhood, and their families were my friends."[5] On August 17th Sukarno heeded their advice and proclaimed Indonesia's independence.

The Dutch, reluctant to surrender their profitable colony, called Sukarno and his men a band of rebels that represented only a radical minority of the people. They enlisted the help of the British to restore order in the Indies under a Dutch flag. Cities around the country were bombed and taken over by British and Dutch forces, but their rule never trickled out to the countryside. Over the course of a four-year revolution more than 45,000 Indonesians were killed, at least sixty-four for every one casualty of Dutch/British forces. But the Indonesian's resolve could not be deterred, and in December of 1949 the Dutch finally surrendered.

Sukarno was never one to relinquish the limelight that came with being Indonesia's first president. He became known to "keep statesmen waiting while he listens patiently to a ragged old woman's complaint."[6] He deported tens of thousands of foreign businessmen, dismantled parliament, declared himself "President for Life," withdrew Indonesia from the United Nations, and in early 1965 declared that year to be "The Year of Living Dangerously," which also became the title for CJ Koch's classic novel and a movie starring Mel Gibson (not as Sukarno).

His insatiable appetite for women could cause one to question his true motivation behind learning so many languages. In his last six years as president alone he married five times. Some of his most notorious lovers included a nineteen year old Japanese geisha, who became his wife, and a blond Russian translator, who was most likely a KGB spy, which Sukarno most likely knew.

Sukarno is remembered for the vision he set for Indonesia in *Pancasila* (Javanese: Five Principles) that still acts as a core foundation of Indonesia's government; 1) Belief in one God (All Indonesians and even temporary residents must check off a religion. Atheism is not an option), 2) Just and Civilized humanity, 3) Indonesian Unity, 4) Democracy and 5) Social Justice. While he was incredibly effective in inspiring an Indonesian national identity and pride into his people, his steps toward dictatorship largely soured his record. He also proved to be inept to the task of growing his country's economy as inflation and cost of living standards soared out of control during his reign.[7]

The CIA brainstormed numerous ways of assassinating Sukarno, and it still unknown to this day what role the U.S. played in the coup of September 30th, 1965 that would push Sukarno from power and allow for the rise of Suharto, a staunch ally of America from LBJ through Clinton. Once during a Sukarno state visit to the White House President Kennedy commented to one of his aides, "No wonder Sukarno doesn't like us very much. He has to sit down with the people who tried to overthrow him."[8]

The most blatant aggression proven to be linked to the US against Sukarno's government took place in the late 1950s simultaneously in the Maluku islands and right here in West Sumatra. Both rebellions were aided by the CIA. I had never met an Indonesian with any involvement in one of these rebellions until a friend from the Belanak's art house took me to his village, deep in the mountains of West Sumatra.

***

Pak (father, title given to much older men) Bactiar Naik sits on the floor of his two room wooden house. There is no furniture. A few frames decorate the otherwise bare walls. A glance outside of *Pak* Naik's window presents one of the serene picturesque views West Sumatra is known for, a dirt road where children, some barely able to walk, move freely and neighbors that are happy to offer avocados off their own tree as you pass through valleys of rice fields leading up to the Barisan Mountain range. Hidden deep in the jungles surrounding these mountains is the history of a time when the people from this province believed, like many other parts of Indonesia believed then and now, that their little province could defeat Indonesia's national army and one day control their own destiny.

There is one picture of each of his two sons and a certificate from the Indonesian government affirming that this meek, old man, weighing maybe 100 pounds sopping wet, worked as a parole officer in a nearby prison. *Pak* Naik is so excited to show me this certificate he almost breaks the rusting frame as he rips it off the wall. There is another act of service *Pak* Naik performed that he never received a certificate for, despite the fact that he risked his life for much of his early-20s supporting its cause.

Bactiar Naik was one of those Indonesians who believed his people, the Minang of West Sumatra, were not getting the attention they deserved from Jakarta to progress. From 1958 through 1961 young men from West Sumatra fought the Indonesian army, mostly deep in their own jungles. There was never an official pronouncement, and many people today believe that the Minang were not necessarily seeking independence, but rather a larger say in the direction of Indonesia. On February 10, 1958 Colonel Ahmat Hussein announced the Sumatran rebel's five-day ultimatum against the central government with a primary demand of Sukarno's cabinet resigning. At hearing his former leader's name *Pak* Naik straightens up, salutes and proclaims "Ahmad Hussein ketuaku!" (Ahmad Hussein is my chief!)

The Eisenhower Administration, which was losing patience with Sukarno and his rebel streak, was more than happy to support any rebel group looking to stir things up in Indonesia. Five weeks prior to West Sumatra's Declaration of War the USS Thomaston accompanied by submarine USS Bluegill docked in Padang to unload 900 pistols, 1,440 submachine guns and 1.3 million rounds of 9-mm ammunition. The arms were unloaded in the middle of the night and moved to strategic posts. Other large shipments of weapons, ammunition and basic livelihood supplies were dropped into these nearby jungles by CIA pilots taking off from Taiwan and the Philippines.

I had been directed to *Pak* Naik's house by members of his village. He seems to be one of the last surviving veterans of this forgotten war. In the first ten minutes of our meeting *Pak* Naik asks me three times if I am with the CIA. Each time he looks over at his wife, who appears to be better fed than himself, and laughs loudly. He finds it ludicrous than an American not involved with the CIA would take the time to find him in *Tanah Garam* (Salty Land), Solak to ask him questions about a regional rebellion that ended fifty years ago.

On March 12, 1958 Indonesian central military launched its first attack to suppress the rebellion. On April 16, 1958 another central government attack was launched, this time with a bit more irony. Colonel Ahmad Yani, a fierce anticommunist who had undergone military training in Kansas, invaded Padang with tactical help from US Army Major George Benson. Benson provided Colonel Yani with Sumatra maps and even helped with parts of the invasion plan. As quoted by Conboy and Morrison in *Times of Indonesia*, "Here was [Yani,] an openly pro-American officer in an anticommunist army ready to carry out a major offensive – with the help of a U.S Army major [Benson]

– against a rebel force supported by a different branch of the American government [the CIA]."[9]

There are two possible explanations for the US's involvement on both sides of a civil war in Indonesia. One would be a complete breakdown of communication between the CIA, the American military and the executive branch. A second and more probable explanation would be that the goal of US foreign policy makers had nothing to do with backing a winner and everything to do with causing havoc. Eisenhower took the position elaborated by the CIA's Deputy Director for Plans, Frank Wisner, "I think it's time we held Sukarno's feet to the fire."[10]

So at the age of 21, Bactiar Naik spent his *merantau* in the nearby jungles fighting against the same Javanese soldiers that less than a decade ago were the Minang's comrades in Indonesia's struggle for independence. He spent three and a half years fighting the troops Jakarta sent after them, kept strong by the white rice grown in their fields and smuggled out to them and by the American AK-47s and hand grenades that had fallen from the sky, gifts to these Minang rebels from one of the world's superpowers that felt Indonesia's President was not taking a strong enough stand against communism. In Eisenhower's own words, "What would a few million dollars do by raising hell in Indonesia if its government started into the communist camp?"

As we yap away, still sitting on the floor, Mr. Naik is still 100% sure that I am a CIA operative. He tells me that an insect crawled into one of his ears, and that he is almost deaf. I make sure to keep my voice raised while asking him questions. While I have the attention of this man who was born in this village when it was part of a Dutch colony, ran the streets as a boy when it was under Japanese occupation, grew up under a new-born Indonesia led by Sukarno and lived most of his adult life under President Suharto, I try to pry some of his opinions on these people who shaped Indonesia.

"The Dutch were cruel. They forced us to pay taxes and gave us nothing. They stole from us. Only the children of very important people could go to school. The Dutch forced us to be stupid people."

"The Japanese made us give them all of our rice. We were forced to eat cassava. I remember the Japanese soldiers always being very drunk and loud."

"I remember Sukarno most for getting our Independence. In his last years, he was persuaded too much by the communists. I did not like when he made himself, 'President for Life'."

"Suharto was a great person. He built roads. He did many things that it took Sukarno too long to do. Suharto introduced pensions for people who worked in police administration like me. And Suharto killed the Communists. If he did not kill them they would have killed us."

Pak Naik's opinions of the Dutch, Japanese and Sukarno are not much different from that of many Indonesians his age. But he spoke more favorably of Suharto, considered to be one of the 20th Century's worst tyrants, than most. It was also interesting to hear that *Pak* Naik and so many Indonesians would have been so afraid of communism. Many Indonesians explain their contempt for communism not on any political or historical grounds, but on the notion that it is godless. As if capitalism was inherently infused with the teachings of Islam.

Old age, sickness, war, starvation, and an insect in his ear may have taken a toll on Bactiar Naik's body, but none have infiltrated his soul. His eyes still radiate the same glow of curiosity as the boys down the road chasing crickets. With his legs crossed and his shoulders swaying as he enthusiastically answers all of my questions, it is easy to picture *Pak* Naik as a brave, young soldier determined to defend his land.

In the fall of 1961, after the rebels had brokered an agreement with the national army, Bactiar Naik and his fellow soldiers walked out of the jungle and back to their hometown. He casually admits, "We never could have defeated Jakarta's powerful army." Their first stop was *Taman Merdeka* (Independence Park), a small playground and field, where early today I saw young children playing soccer. On this field, the national soldiers had the rebels sign their names to a scroll of paper and then line up to have their photos taken in groups of five. They were not home long before it was time to find a job. Many, like *Pak* Naik, found work in some form of police administration. Others just went back to work in the rice fields. Many more rebels enlisted in the national army that they had just finished fighting.

I thank *Pak* Naik for his time and he shakes my hand heartily with both of his hands. After taking a few pictures with him and his wife, *Pak* Naik stands waving in front of his house. Before I am out of an ear shot's distance, which is not very far, I shout, *"CIA mengucapkan terima kasih anda terlalu!"* (The CIA thanks you too!). *Pak* Naik's eyes almost pop out of his head, and he quickly runs inside to tell his wife that he was right.

***

From the top of *Bukit* Padang I look down on the domes of Padang's mosques, the different colored *angkuts* (taxi vans) zipping around the bustling streets and the imposing malls. The mountains rise up to Andalas University where once I had an office with a sign on the door that read "Visiting Professor," and the Indian Ocean washes the sand at Padang's beaches where I religiously watched every sunset I could.

Looking off the other cliff there is a trail I ran some mornings before the temperature rose too high. I would finish on the grooved shore of *Pantai Air Manis* (Sweet Water Beach), where I would drop in to see my unfortunate friend, Malin Kundang. Malin grew up in these parts and became a sailor. After acquiring a small

44

fortune and marrying a princess, Malin returned to *Pantai Air Manis,* but refused to recognize his impoverished mother who raised him. Legend has it that his mother begged God to turn her son into a stone and God complied. So after every run I sit alone for a few minutes on the shore with this stone of a small man prostrating himself with his face in the sand. (If you pry locals for a more rational explanation of how and when this stone was created they will look at you like you have three heads.)

A few months before my trip began I met Erick Setiawan, a gifted Indonesian-born story teller living in California, who named my favorite character in his first novel after Malin Kundang. Like tens of millions of Indonesians he has never seen Malin for himself, but only listened to his mother recount his fate. His mother's stories were a major influence in Setiawan's writing. It was at times like that when I realized how intimate a picture of Indonesia I was experiencing.

The feelings I have atop *Bukit* Padang are not all contented ones. Padang, with a population of almost one million, is one of the places on earth most likely to be devastated by the next tsunami. Many scientists and engineers agree that there is no question of "if" but only "when." With a local and national government that have not taken even the most basic preparations on behalf of its people, like posting signs for an evacuation route, a tsunami in Padang is bound to take thousands of lives with it. The word "Padang" will dominate the nightly news reels for a brief time. People around the world will give generously from their hearts millions of dollars. Hundreds of international NGOs will rush in to aid a smaller population of people that with just a bit of preparation could have easily been spared the loss of many loved ones.

I wonder if someone will stand, right where I am, on *Bukit* Padang when it happens and film it for the world. That warm tide rolling in, what will it look two storeys high? The shores which welcomed American ammunition in the 1950s and bid farewell to Malin Kundang long before he became a folklore legend, how quickly will they stretch across *Pasar Seni*, and how long will it be before I know who has and has not been accounted for?

Pasar Seni, Padang

Solak, West Sumatra

2

South Sumatra

We had driven from Ventimiglia to Piso and Florence, across the Romagna to Rimini, back through Forli, Imola, Bologna, Parma, Piacenza, and Genoa, to Ventimiglia again. The whole trip had taken only ten days. Naturally, in such a short trip, we had no opportunity to see how things were with the country or the people.

-Ernest Hemingway, Men Without Women

I have less than ten days to cover over 800 miles from Padang to the Jakarta Airport before my visa expires again. And although I have never seen South Sumatra, I find it hard to get excited about this leg of the trip. Even before I begin my first twelve hour bus ride to the town closest to Mount Kerinci, the highest point in Sumatra, the trip feels long and pointless. There are some interesting spots along the way, but I am not giving myself enough time to feel settled anywhere. I arrive in the middle of the night and after knocking on the door of a few hostels I learn quickly enough that the closest town to Sumatra's highest point is not the friendliest place in Indonesia.

I check into a dark overpriced, 100,000 rupiah ($10) room with one window and a view of a concrete wall. There is an arrow in my room with the word, *Kiblat* written under it. I look it up in my dictionary. The hotel wants me to know which direction Mecca is. In the opposite direction is New York, where both of my parents and my oldest niece will all celebrate birthdays this week. Just a few minutes after my weary body passes out, the shrieking sound of the call to prayer pierces through my room. The mosque is only a few feet away, and I fight to fall back asleep.

There is something devastating about a town whose main source of income is to cut down all of its trees and truck them out. It feels as if whatever life exists is in a constant state of depletion. The looks on locals' faces lack any discernible emotion, not even a drop of surprise or interest at the *bule* walking their streets. All those trees must be sold for some profit, but I could not find it. Instead I just watched passing bundles of logs roped down to the backs of truck after truck kicking dirt into the air.

I buy an apple and bread and take it back to my hotel. I already have some peanut butter in my bag. I order a cold drink from the hotel restaurant and ask for a knife to make my sandwich. A fork and spoon are the common table settings in Indonesia. That is when hands are not being used. After a few minutes an old man returns and hands me a rusted box cutter. I manage to cut my apple the best I can with the handle of my fork.

That night I take a long walk around town. There is a dark field and a couple guys, probably mid-20s, hanging out on the bleachers. They look over at me, and I can tell they are building up the courage to get the *bule's* attention. Usually there are three reasons why locals would stop a foreigner walking by; to practice their English, to have a conversation where they hope to learn about you and the place you are from and possibly teach you something about their land or to have a good laugh at the way you look, dress and speak.

"Hello! Mau ke mana?" (Where are you going?)

"Jalan-Jalan." (Taking a walk/ Out and about/ most common response to *Mau ke mana?*)

I wave and keep walking.

"Mau Bir?" (Want Beer?) I do a quick 180 and join my new friends on the bleachers.

What we drink is not actually beer, but a bitter wine. It must be from some local fruit. We drink out of a clear plastic bag with a rubber band tightly wrapped around two protruding straws. Didi and Rico are both locals and like drinking.

"Your President Osama..." Rico embarrassed, knows he messed up and looks to Didi to help him out, "Your President Obama. He (makes a shooting motion with his hand) Osama."

Since bin Laden's death a week ago, a number of Indonesians have raised the topic as if congratulating me on my hometown winning a game. I nod yes and try to change the subject. Didi eyes light up, "You like Indonesian girls?"

"Of course, Indonesian girls are beautiful."

"Ahhhhhhhhhhhhh!"

Didi and Rico squirm around, slapping each other on the back. "We have lots of lady friends. Want to meet?"

I can already imagine what line of work Didi and Rico's lady friends are in, but I remember a piece of advice a Californian writer I met in Toba gave me, "Write every day and just keep putting yourself in as many precarious situations as possible."

The three of us hop on one motorbike. We wobble down the dimly lit street and park in front of a mall. My friend Desmon has an interesting philosophy on malls. He calls them a cancer to Indonesia. He said they go up all over the country, and they are filled with all these things most people can not afford and never thought about buying. Then they start thinking about what they need to do to be able to shop in one of these malls. Naturally, they become unhappy.

The mall is closed. The metal security gates have been pulled down, but a side door is still open and there is a faint sound of Asian pop music coming from a far corner. Didi and Rico stop to urinate on one of the gates. The mall is dark and empty except for a few stray cats. We walk up to a restaurant with Anker and Guinness Beer on display. There are some CDs taped to the wall, a middle-aged woman standing behind the counter and a stern guy off to the side wearing a security shirt and a gold-colored belt with a long knife tucked into it.

We walk into the back room with cheap multi-colored blinking lights and sit down on a couple beat up couches. Didi takes an Anker bottle and a Guinness can and begins mixing them. Rico lights up a cigarette and starts singing karaoke into a muffled speaker system. Talana walks in wearing jeans, a lot of make-up and a tight shirt that says "Doing It." She sits next to me. She is originally from the town I taught in so we have enough to talk about. She was married for a couple years. She shows me a picture of her little girl. She works in a salon during the day hair styling and giving massages. At night she works here. She hardly ever goes back to Padang.

She asks me vague questions about America and tries to seem interested in my answers. She doesn't smile and does not flirt in any way. Rico, who has a girl sitting next to him now, asks me with a big cheese on his face if I like her.

"Dia cantik." (She is beautiful.)

In between the karaoke songs that are now being sung by another prostitute, I start making my exit. I put 40,000 rupiah ($4.00) on the table for the drinks. I shake hands with Didi and Rico who are noticeably disappointed that I am not hanging out longer. I thank them for introducing me to their friends. I kiss Talana and her friend on the cheek goodbye. Talana's friend pouts and says *"Mau cium di bibir."* (Want kiss on the lips.) I pretend to not understand and wave goodbye to the room. On the way out I exchange nods with the security guard, and I am on high alert until I get outside of the mall.

As I walk back to my hotel I think about my cousins, aunts, uncles and all my other family at home celebrating my Mom's 70th birthday tonight.

***

Before dawn, I am shaken out of bed by the prayerful tremors pulsating from the mosque. I realize that I am not excited about hiking to the highest point in Sumatra or in anything else this town has to offer. I pack up my things and decide to find a bus that will take me anywhere else. In a surprising start to my day, the receptionist only charges me for one night, even though I have not even voiced a complaint.

Back at sea level, the next town is Bengkulu. The beaches have the same view as Padang, but with gentler waves and no panhandlers. I shed my sneakers and take a long walk along the ocean's shoreline that is much needed after a 13 ½ hour bus ride.

I find some former Dutch and British forts. The British dabbled in South Sumatra creating a pepper colony that lasted from 1685 until 1824, but never turned out much of a profit. They finally ceded it to the Dutch so that they could concentrate on their colonies in Malacca (present-day Malaysia). There is also a museum of the house where President Sukarno once resided. In the 1930s Sukarno lived in Bengkulu as a prisoner of war under the Dutch. After walking around the tranquil grounds of Sukarno's Bengkulu estate I can see that he did not have the roughest POW experience. In Bengkulu, Sukarno met his third wife, Fatmawati, the mother of Megawati Sukarnopurti who became Indonesia's fifth president, and first female head of state in 1999.

I stop in at an open-air barber shop with a long mirror across the side wall. The barber, Tony, a young guy with hair more stylish than his clothes charges 10,000 ($1) for a haircut that includes a free shoulder rub at the end. After answering Tony's initial, more typical questions (country, age, marital status, reason I am in Indonesia) he dives into a topic that is a little deeper and seems to be a source of wonder for all Indonesians. He wants to know my thoughts on *nasi* (rice).

"Do you eat *nasi?*"

"Of course, I have been in Asia for almost four years now."

"Do you eat rice for *makan pagi?*" (breakfast, literally: morning food)

"No, I would rather eat anything else in the morning, but I often eat it for lunch and dinner."

And now here comes the big question.

"Do they have *nasi* in America?"

"Yes, Americans do not eat rice nearly as much as Asians, but you can buy it at any supermarket. You can also find Chinese restaurants all over America."

Tony goes back to cutting my hair with a big grin on his face. If there is ever a boom in the haircut business and he is able to save enough for a trip to America he will not have to worry finding his favorite food. It makes me feel like someone up there must be looking out for us when things work out like this. With all of that *nasi* growing all over Asia and a lack of so many other delicious foods, the fact that every Asian I meet loves their *nasi* as much as this guy is somewhat of a miracle. Just imagine how much negative tension would be added to earth if Asians hated rice.

Another patron walks in and takes a seat.

"*Sudah makan?*" (Have you eaten?)

"Sudah" (I have).

The question, "Have you eaten?" is actually a common greeting in many parts of Southeast Asia. In a land where clinical depression has not yet spread and complaining is something they watch white people do in movies, "have you eaten?" is just as appropriate a question as "how are you doing?"

Still in the barber's seat, Tony gives me a quick, violent backrub. At this point I have spent at least three quarters of the 85 hours I will spend on Sumatran busses, and he seems to know how to throw my bones back to where they belong. For one dollar Tony gives as good a haircut as any barber I have visited. I have gotten other hair cuts in Asia that were such a disaster they ended up as screensavers on my friends' cell phones back home. I say goodbye and stop at the first place I can find selling *nasi goreng* (fried rice).

***

I leave Bengkulu without making any real cultural observations except that the women seem to have fuller lips than girls from the rest of the country. Still, I am glad I made the stop to let out a small bit of my crankiness. There is enough restlessness left inside me, and I do not want to spend my birthday tomorrow in a crowded city. There is a town called Krui that Lonely Planet writes a few sentences about, "Quiet coastal village. . . unspoilt coastline. . . magnificent scenery. . . well off the beaten track." None of my friends in Padang have ever heard of this town, which I like.

The bus is long and rusting on the inside and outside. Everyone on the bus is smoking away. We stop about once every three to three and a half hours and after having ample time to eat, go to the bathroom and smoke a half dozen cigarettes while walking around in the fresh air, the first thing everyone does – after we all get our butts squeezed in – is light up a cigarette. Most Indonesians smoke *kreteks*, hand-wrapped, clove-flavored cigarettes that burn longer and contain almost four times the amount of tar and nicotine as ordinary cigarettes.

I should not be surprised considering we are not far from 2010's YouTube sensation "Smoking Baby." Ardi Razal, two years old at the time, became famous world-wide as the baby who smokes two packs of cigarettes a day. Millions watched this ridiculously fat cheeked toddler blowing smoke rings, juggling a cigarette with three fingers and lighting up the next cigarette with the one in his mouth. His parents claim that if they do not give him cigarettes he pounds his head against the floor.

Two-thirds of Indonesian men smoke, which actually sounds to me like a low estimate. According to the World Health Organization, smoking claims 425,000 Indonesian lives every year, nearly a quarter of the country's annual death toll. Contrary to world trends smoking is on the rise in Indonesia due mainly to the fact that the government does absolutely nothing to stop it. There is no minimum age limit on smoking or buying cigarettes. Giant cigarette billboards are audaciously plastered along most major roads. It is rare to see a television commercial break without at least one smoking advertisement. Ninety percent of Indonesian children under the age of ten have watched a cigarette commercial, which makes me believe that the other ten percent have never watched TV. Indonesia's basketball leagues are filled with teenagers toting *Djarum's L.A. Lights* t-shirts. Little Ardi is probably one of the biggest tourist attractions in these parts, but I doubt I would have much fun spending my 29th birthday with a smoking baby.

The 40-seater *Krui Putra* bus slows down on a deserted road. A clean shaven, young guy with a small backpack jumps in through the back door. The bus does not even make a complete stop. He grabs a seat next to me. We nod at each other and about three hours later, after he still does not light up a *kretek,* I start a conversation with him.

"Where are you going?"

"Jakarta!" he says with a big innocent smile, rolling the "*r*" with youthful pride.

"What's going on in Jakarta?"

"I have a job there."

"Oh yeah, doing what?"

Lifting his chin up high, "I will be a driver."

I can tell he has been dying to tell someone why he is on this bus since he hopped on, and I can feel the enthusiasm vibrating off his words. It is hard to think of a job I would hate more than driving around Jakarta's notoriously suicidal rush hour jams. But hey, to each his own, right?

"Do you like Jakarta?"

"I have never been. A friend from my hometown called and said there was a job. This is my first time leaving my hometown."

"Does your family live where you were picked up."

"No, I walked a long way because the bus driver does not charge you as much if you get on the bus in between towns."

I look over at this baby-faced kid with his impassioned eyes and self-assured voice. He just left everything he knows with a small backpack and hopped on this dirty rusting bus that did not even make a complete stop for him, and in about 40 hours after a ferry cruise and another bus ride he will arrive in the capital of his country and begin his life.

He loves Harry Potter books and American movies. He says it would be a dream come true to see Hollywood and the White House. His name is Gusti, which he says means prince. I try to remember if my own picture of Herman Hesse's young *Siddhartha* would look much different. Gusti might be just a little skinnier. His unyielding optimism takes me back to being twenty-two when I got every last mile out of that old Ford Escort to take my first job teaching in an inner-city Texas school. Or even eighteen, when my parents drove me to college in their '89 Chrysler Fifth Avenue. Such different places, circumstances and wheels, but still that same spirit that nothing could touch you, the youthful pride in not having a clue where life will take you, judging every person you meet as extraordinary if only because each has earned a part in your life story. So full of yourself and life and so obsessed with the line on a map that traces where it all began and could be going.

Gusti stared out his window at the passing trees and began speaking slowly. He sounded less like he was talking to me and more like he was narrating the movie that would one day be made about his life, portraying that moment.

"Leaving everyone I know... for *Jakarrrrta*...Maybe in five years I will return home with a lot of money."

And then in a long exhaling breath, an English word that most people know from television commercials.

"SUCCESS!"

I envied Gusti in that moment. I envied his outlook, the fascination he held in his own life. How do you hold on to it, through the strings of Monday mornings, humbling setbacks and all the sour smoke that enters your lungs from other people's mouths? I wondered if Gusti could hold on to it and when I lost it.

We exchanged phone numbers and emails. Although I doubt Gusti checks his email very often. We shook hands and wished each other good luck. The bus pulled into Krui earlier than scheduled, which made me feel like things were looking up. The bus even made a complete stop for me.

I stepped off into a new city that no one I knew had ever been to. I had been feeling slightly guilty about rushing the last couple cities. I remember when I first started travelling how every place was exotic. I was like a simple dumb-witted boy from the country side, impressed with every street and view, excited to talk to anyone; every street vendor, taxi driver and bum I could find. But being overseas for years had robbed me of the thrill that came with walking the streets of a new city for the first time. If I was in Argentina or France no one would know purely by the sight of me that I was not a local, unless they just deemed me to be too unfashionable to have been born there. But in Asia, all it takes is one glance at my blue eyes and sunburned face standing a full head taller than every crowd to know I do not belong. And all of the attention I had received had made me defensive. I did not want to recite my nationality, age, marital status and opinion of Indonesia to every person I met any longer, but I was also holding myself back from experiencing Indonesia, which was supposed to be the point of this whole trip. I needed to go back to looking at everything as a kid would. I needed to be more like Gusti.

***

I wake up the next morning at the Sampana Hotel with another year under my belt and a lot of mosquito bites on my feet. For 65,000 rupiah ($6.50) a night I am sleeping in one of the more drab rooms of the trip, but just a stone's throw from the beach. I make myself a peanut butter and apple sandwich and go out to start my day. Before I leave the hotel the girl working the desk has two messages for me: the owner of the hotel wants to buy some of my jewelry and the local police are looking for me.

After getting settled into my room last night I went for a *jala-jalan* around Krui and met a handful of gentlemen that were very interested in my life story. I told them how I had given up teaching to start my own pearl jewelry business at home in New York, that I go to lakes in China to buy pearls and that I make most of my meager salary for the year during the Christmas Season, which is why I have a deadline to finish this trip. Since stones are popular in Indonesia, I traded a lot of pearls with a Brazillian friend for stone jewelry before leaving New York.

They asked if I had any to show. Since I never want to leave my jewelry in a hotel and I always want to be ready to make a sale, I laid a few pieces out on a bench. After some light bargaining, half a dozen men went home with gifts to give to their wives and

63

daughters, and I had enough rupiah to pay for the next few days of my trip.

Apparently word gets around fast in Krui. The owner did not want his wife to be the only woman in town without a piece of pearl or stone jewelry from the *bule* and the cops wanted their cut, which could easily mean taking all of my jewelry and rupiah and a lot of empty threats of moving me to a free room in an Indonesian prison.

After selling a bracelet to the owner, I walk over to Venus' shop. Venus is one of my customers from the night before. He said that there is an American that has been living along the beach of this town for the last fifteen years with his Javanese wife and child. He offered to take me to meet him today.

Venus' store is a wooden structure, similar to a small clubhouse, extending from the front of his house and facing Krui's main road. You have to holler into the house to get someone's attention. Venus comes out and introduces me to his wife and two daughters. He has a couple big fish in each of his hands that he caught early that morning. He says that the American is out of town, but he wants the two of us to go cook these fish on the beach. With long hair, a healthy build and a Rolling Stones seat on his motorbike, Venus seems to be in constant chill mode.

I ride on the back of his motorbike and we park under a row of palm trees. We gather up some sticks and leaves and Venus gets a fire going. *Ikan Bakar* (literally: burnt fish) is one of my favorite meals. The fish is not actually burnt, but the skin is charred giving it a black appearance that is later doused with an orange sauce. A woman comes out of a nearby house to ask if we need anything and later returns with two plates of *nasi* and the orange sauce, which we forgot. Venus insists that she accept a fish for her generosity.

The meal is as good as any I have had on the trip. Venus refuses to take any money from me to pay for the fish or even the *bensin* (gasoline) after he drives me to see Krui's sites, an old British cannon standing atop a cliff facing the ocean and a paved runway where someday Krui will have its own airport. We also ride to an abandoned cabin in the woods that belonged to Venus' late father-in-law. The surrounding rubber trees are being tapped for latex, which drips out in a white liquid. He says he would like to fix it up so that his family will have a quiet retreat outside of town.

That night Venus, still unaware that it is my birthday, asks me where I want to go. We drive along the shore until we find Obama's Hotel & Bar and my birthday wish of being able to drink beer and speak English is fulfilled. There are a few foreigners drinking bottles of *Bintang* (Star) beer on an outdoor deck. There are two surfers, one from Australia and another from Spain and a chubby Frenchman who was told by his employer in France to take a three year holiday due to the economic crisis. He has been hitchhiking and riding his bike for twenty-one months through Europe and Siberia and down China and Southeast Asia. He says

Indonesians are the most intrusive people he has ever met.

Earlier in the day a wild boar emerged from the jungle and tore through this beach town sending the locals into a flurry. It was finally harpooned to death. Since barbecued boar happens to fall on the list of forbidden Muslim foods, it is up to the Aussie, Frenchie, Spaniard, Argentine hotel owner and myself to devour all of this good meat. The Aussie plays a few songs on the guitar and Venus plays his favorite, *Honky Tonk Woman*. Like so many Indonesians, Venus is a natural on the guitar. He is a little shy singing, but still surprises me since I did not think he could speak English at all. The night ends up turning into a memorable birthday full of backpacker stories, live rock music, good beer and boar.

The next morning I meet a local teacher and head out to a public high school to talk to a classroom of teenagers about my trip. When I return to my hotel I get the same message, which is beginning to alarm me, "the cops came by looking for you." An old man sitting in the lobby adds a new twist to it, "They asked if you are selling marijuana?" No foreigners go to Indonesia to sell marijuana. The risk is too high and the profit margin is too low considering natives are perfectly capable of growing it themselves. I know this. The old man knows it, and of course the cops do as well. The cops must be hatching a plan to plant marijuana on me. It hits me how I would be the perfect victim. They already have eyewitnesses that can testify that I was making some sort of transactions on the street.

In Indonesia the police are seldom looked at by anyone as a defender of law and order. Here are a few quotes from civilians describing their police force, "When you choose to deal with the police you are only making yourself a victim." "Any imbecile can become a cop. They just borrow money from their friends and family to pay the fee (as much as 40 million rupiah or US$4,000) and then as soon as they become cops they use their power to make that money back." And my personal favorite, "If you get robbed and you feel like getting robbed twice, just call the police."

Veteran backpackers all give the same advice, "If you are caught breaking the law, pay the first bribe." A cop on the street may extort you for $200. By the time that cop takes you to see his captain the bribe will likely have tripled, and by the time the case gets to a judge the bribe could easily be tens of thousands of U.S. dollars.

I decide to not let it get to that point. Fifteen minutes later my bag is packed, and I am sipping tea with Venus waiting for the next bus to take me further south. Venus was kind enough to go to the terminal and purchase my ticket. He says that he can wave the bus down when it gets to his house. After reimbursing him for the ticket, Venus still refuses to take any money for gas or food. I hand him a pair of pearl earrings to give to his wife. He gives me the sternest look I have seen in Sumatra and asks "Friends?" I assure him that of course it is a gift between friends and not out of debt.

A rusting 40-seater *Krui Putra* bus, which looks exactly like the rusting 40-seater *Krui Putra* bus I arrived on, makes a complete stop in front of Venus' house. There is one seat left in the back row. I throw my backpack in the aisle and squeeze into it. Venus, his wife and daughters wave good-bye. I get one last peek at the Krui shoreline where I spent one of my more memorable birthdays. I feel rejuvenated and ready to explore the southern tip of Sumatra. I do not even mind too much the old man next to me ashing his *kretek* on my backpack, and the first seven of a fourteen-hour bus ride flies by.

***

The shore of *Pulau Anak Krakatau* (Child of Krakatau Island) is so black I feel as if I am walking on soot from a recent fire, soot as soft as snow. The crystal clear waves break gently along its beach. Just a few steps inland there is a narrow grove of pine trees that ends just before the ashy land begins to rise sharply to a height of almost 1,100 feet (as of 2011). The thin patch of green seems to contain the sole life on the island. Unless, like some locals living a banana boat ride away, you believe that the raging fires and smoldering lava beneath it are alive.

Anak Krakatau owes its name to a much larger volcano that rose from the very same place in the Sunda Straits before she blew her lid and herself to pieces in

August of 1883. Krakatau was the fifth largest volcanic eruption in the Earth's history and the deadliest one to date. For nearly 21 continuous hours Krakatau spewed and roared sending six cubic miles of rock and ash up to fifty miles into the atmosphere and letting herself be heard nearly 3,000 miles away, making the loudest sound in modern history. At least 165 Indonesian villages were regarded as completely devastated and more than 36,000 people died. Deaths were caused by burning, sulphur-dioxide poisoning, but most were a result not of the actual eruption, but from the ensuing 100-foot tsunamis.

In *Krakatoa: The Day the World Exploded*, Simon Winchester raises the idea that the eruption and utter poverty and misery that followed may have acted as a catalyst for anti-colonialist sentiment as well as opening the door in Java to militant Islam. A more easily traced effect of Krakatau was the sunsets that were seen around the world for years to follow. Firefighters in New York and Connecticut raced toward horizons of furious, blood reds, iridescent gold and every possible colorful tone in between only to learn that the fire they were chasing was on the other side of the world. The billions of tons of ash and debris still floating deep in the atmosphere affected sunsets on every continent for years to come, inspiring some of the most soulful work of art and poetry of the time.

The island I am standing on, *Anak Krakatau*, is actually the caldera of Krakatau. *Anak* Krakatau emerged above water in 1927 and has been growing rapidly ever since. It is currently growing at a rate of sixteen feet per year. The two old seamen I hired for the ride have left me here with a teenage tour guide who knows nothing about Krakatau or *Anak* Krakatau. There is a wooden billboard listing all prohibited behaviors at *Anak* Krakatau and threatening that they will be fully enforced by the park ranger. As far as I can see there is no park ranger or any other human beings to be found on *Anak* Krakatau's shoreline.

As we step through the grove of trees I hear something moving near us, and I just hope that it is not a snake. Fortunately, instead a four-foot lizard stops in his tracks and looks at us. I am nearly positive that it is a Komodo dragon, which I recognize from a Marlon Brando movie. I did not expect to see komodo dragons until reaching islands on the other side of Java, and I was not expecting to get this close. He starts whipping his slithery tongue in the air, which I take as a threat, but is actually his way of smelling out dead or dying animals that could be miles away. Translated as simply lizard, *biawaks* are the slightly smaller, less aggressive cousins of Komodo dragons. My tour guide, not nearly as impressed with the *biawak* as I am, continues leading me up the volcano.

We pass a few short, scorched trees that did not survive the more recent minor eruptions. Another sign of those eruptions are the scatterings of rocks that were hurled from the mouth of *Anak* Krakatau and the resulting craters around them. The barren landscape and sheer desolation gives me a sensation of walking on the moon. The hike up would not be physically strenuous if it were not for the unforgiving sun and the heat which intensifies with each ascending footprint I plant. About halfway up I realize that the incline we are on comes to a peak that is not the caldera of the volcano. Instead the land slopes abruptly downward, where white sulphur deposits have built up, before rising back up toward the crater's rim. My tour guide informs me that it is much too dangerous to walk all the way to the crater's rim. Krakatau's last series of eruptions ended five months before my journey here and the next series would begin four months after we get back on our little boat.

Looking almost straight across at Krakatau's peak, I pause for a few moments allowing the sweat to spill off my body into one puddle. The climb and the views, while picturesque enough, were not quite as dramatic as I had imagined. The allure came less from what my eyes saw and more from the history behind this cone of land, born from a mother who threw one of the most devastating tantrums known to man. The thrill came from standing atop an island mountain that was born around the same time as my favorite college professor. It came from imagining blazing lava rise straight up to the heavens from this exact spot and seeing that spectacle reflected off the eyes of fisherman, merchants, Dutch colonialists, mothers and children. It came from the rumors of those exceptionally exotic sunsets that if I was alive I could have watched right from my childhood park.

And then on the walk down my mind, as if just itching to make a wise-ass comment on behalf of my body, recalled a Mark Twain quote about the simpletons who add to their list of things which they have seen and other people have not by climbing "unnecessarily the perilous peaks. . . and derive no pleasure from it except the reflection that it isn't a common experience."

***

On my walk home from a *warnet* (internet café) that night I buy some fried tempeh and run into some older guys hanging around outside of a store. They call me over to sit down, and I join them. When they hear I am American, they excitedly tell me that my president went to school in Indonesia.

They offer me plates of chicken *sate* (strips of meat cooked in peanut oil and eaten off skewers) and a plastic bottle filled with *anggur* (wine). I ask if there is any alcohol in the *anggur*, which is being passed around in two small glasses. They say no, it just helps them sleep. They also claim the wine makes them strong as they flex their muscles. As opposed to Catholics, who can at times seem to disagree with the entire Bible, the Muslims I have met do not like to admit they disagree with or do not obey any word of the Koran. They keep the wine in a plastic Aqua bottle, instead of the original glass bottle so the cops do not bother them. I tell them my story about being on the run from the Krui cops and receive affirming nods all around.

I must have started a trend because one by one each of the guys tells a story that makes him seem a little more important, a little more of a man. Most of the stories involve women that naturally fell hard for the storyteller. A slightly more modest gentleman in his fifties speaks very softly about his wife and three daughters. Whenever he mentions a daughter he smiles widely and pulls at one earlobe to stress to me that she is a girl. His story ends up being drowned out by the others shouting and making sex motions with their hands. There is the typical right pointer finger going through a hole made with the left hand and the South Sumatran favorite of two hands flapping together like a fish.

The oldest and most vocal is a 61-year-old veteran of Indonesia's *Tantara* (Army). He spent thirty-one years stationed across the archipelago, mainly keeping watch over separatist rebel groups in Aceh, Kalimantan, Papua and East Timor. He was in East Timor in 1975, during one of the Suharto Regime's worst atrocities. When I ask him what it was like in East Timor, he jumps out of his seat and places his hands to look like he is still holding his AK-47. Then he imitates sounds of gunfire and pretends to be mowing down everything in front of him. I am sure neither he nor the other five men would have guessed that I know the story of what happened in East Timor. It is not the same one that they were told by the Suharto regime.

The Portuguese were the first Europeans to leave a mark on the Indies. From roughly 1400-1600 the king and queen of Portugal considered almost all of present-day Indonesia to be its colony. They were later ejected by local kings and the Dutch. However the eastern half of one island, *Timor* (literally: East), was the lone sliver of the Indies the Portuguese held on to until 1975. When they did relinquish their colony, Suharto was determined to seize control of it before its people could declare sovereignty and let the world recognize it with such a ridiculous name as *East Timor* (East East).

Henry Kissinger, Secretary of State under President Ford, met with President Suharto in Jakarta on December 6, 1975, just one day before Indonesia's invasion of the former Portuguese colony. Unwilling to upset a Cold War ally, Kissinger gave Suharto the green light saying, "It is important that whatever you do succeeds quickly."[11] According to Amnesty International, by 1999 when the United Nations forced Indonesia to relinquish its military presence in East Timor, an estimated 200,000 people, one-third of East Timor's population, were killed.

The Suharto regime censored any negative reporting on East Timor from reaching the Indonesian public. Following a 1991 massacre where Indonesian soldiers opened fire on a funeral procession, killing more than 250 unarmed civilians, Seno Gumira Ajidarma wrote *Jazz Perfume and the Incident*. In this delicately constructed book, Ajidarma tells three stories in rotating chapters. One story line follows the history of and inspiration behind jazz, a metaphor for freedom. Another story line dives into the narrator's confusing love life filled with rants about feelings of lust and guilt in both heterosexual and homosexual attractions (possibly another metaphor for freedom). And in the most provocative story, the narrator describes in vivid detail an "incident" that occurs in an unnamed place where innocent men, women and children are raped, tortured and murdered by military officers as the media is shackled from informing the rest of the country. The novel was published in Indonesia and escaped censors because it was categorized as fiction, and because names and dates are omitted. However, in one chapter's closing line Ajidarma goes so far as to state the date of Miles Davis's death in 1991, claiming it was "only forty-eight days before the gunning-down of the unarmed civilians I wrote about earlier".

My friends at this corner store front in Kalianda complain that the people of East Timor are selfish and ungrateful, just like the Acehnese and Papuans. They do not want to share their natural resources with the rest of their countrymen, whose parent's generation fought the Dutch for their freedom. The men around me do not realize that many people within these minority groups look at Indonesia's national government as being no less oppressive and having no more of a right to govern than their previous Dutch rulers.

The men talk about East Timor as a sad place, not because of the people who were killed, but because it broke away. They feel this ungrateful half of an island broke the unity of their proud chain of land. The only acceptable opinion under Suharto, and still popular today, is that from Sabang (Indonesia's most geographically western island in Aceh) to Marauke (Indonesia's most eastern city in Papua) Indonesians are and should be proud to be Indonesians. Ironically the two provinces they quote are the two that most vehemently want to break away.

They speak about East Timor and present day suppressed rebellions, entirely unaware of the rest of the world's views. They have not read what I have read. Most likely neither they nor their children will ever see Aceh or Papua unless they go decked in a camouflaged uniform with a gun hoisted to their hip. The old man that is sharing *anggur* and stories with me is content with his years of service. "I went to East Timor because it was *rusak* (broken)." I can see that I am in another corner of the world where no one has a clue who the good guys or the bad guys are. With all my reading, traveling and analyzing, I can not say I know either.

As the night goes on we talk of lighter subjects that do not include rebellions or massacres. At one point everyone feels a need to show me their identification cards. One line on each of their ID's reads "*Mata: Biasa*" (Eyes: Normal). This cracks me up. The more we drink the more they tell me that this crew is like a family, and that I am now a part of it.

The old veteran starts challenging me to *sate* eating contests. He rips four strips of beef and chicken off their sticks in one bite. As the sauces pour down his cheek, he throws the sticks on the floor, gulps his wine and thumps his chest with his fist. I politely refuse his challenge and assure him that he won. We open another bottle. One guy grabs a handful of ice and puts it in my drink. Indonesians are happy to drink anything at room temperature, but usually assume that a *bule* prefers iced drinks. The old man goes to take a piss and returns with his wiener sticking out of the open zipper of his pants. Everyone yells for him to put it away. I ask the owner of the shop again,

"You sure there is no alcohol in this wine?"

"Oh no, of course not."

The old guy gets on his motorbike and drives in big wobbly circles in the middle of the street. Then he speeds right through our circle, trying to run over the guy who spoke so sweetly about his daughters. He refuses to leave until someone agrees to take a ride to his house. The other guys argue over who will go until the owner, at his wit's end, yells at one of his friends to just get on the bike. I look at the owner with a smirk. Before I can ask one last time he mutters, "*tigabelas persen saja* (just thirteen percent)."

I thank all the guys for a great night and offer a few bucks for the drinks and food. The owner pushes my wallet back into my pocket. They all tell me that the next time I come to Kalianda I must come back to this corner to hang out and drink more *anggur* with them. If I ever make it back to Kalianda, I will.

Krakatau

Krui, South Sumatra

Kantor Imigrasi
Kuala Lumpur, Malaysia

Although Malaysians speak basically the same language and share many customs with Indonesians, Kuala Lumpur is a city unlike any you will find in Indonesia. The streets are smoothly paved and well lit with traffic signs that drivers, more in cars than motorbikes, obey. The lights from the Petronas Twin Towers shine down over a clean city that has a sense of order. Malaya, as it was called in the colonial days, was controlled by the British. The Brits seem to have invested more into their colony than the Dutch did in theirs.

From the armed conflicts of Sukarno's presidency to the threats of war and political posturing that still exist today, tensions run high between these two countries. Malaysia, which has a population one eighth of Indonesia's holds a Gross National Income of US$6,540 per capita, four times that of Indonesia. Malaysians are known to look down on their southern neighbors as if they are their estranged cousins still living in the jungle. Indonesians resent Malaysia for never having to shed revolutionary blood, since Britain peacefully surrendered its colony in 1957. Malaysia's thriving tourism industry often stakes claim to batik painting and shadow puppet theater as well as traditional songs and foods with disputable origins.

Indonesians see this as a classless pillaging of their greatest cultural triumphs. If I ever want to provoke an Indonesian all I have to say is that *rendang* (beef and fried rice mixed with spices and a brown coconut milk sauce) is my favorite Malaysian dish.

Underneath the veneer of a thriving Southeast Asian economy, Malaysia does have plenty of its own problems. At the time of my trip, Anwar Ibrahim, the main opposition leader of Malaysia's Prime Minister, is on trial for having sex with a former male aide. If convicted he could be whipped and thrown in prison for twenty years. This is the second time Anwar Ibrahim has been brought up on accusations of sodomy, which he claims are politically motivated and fabricated by the ruling party. The obsession with trying a politician for a crime like this is ironic because a guy can not walk Kuala Lumpur's main strip without being cat-called by a half dozen transvestite prostitutes.

Just a 50-minute flight from Padang and a two hour flight from Jakarta, Kuala Lumpur has been a convenient foreign city for me to apply for new visas. Even while I was teaching at the university, Padang's *Kantor Imigrasi* would deport me every sixty days and the university would fund my trip here. I was usually able to find flights with Air Asia, whose billboards and advertisements are filled with some of the sexiest women in Asia wearing tight red uniforms, for 10,000-50,000 rupiah ($10-$50). But a pleasant, affordable flight with gorgeous stewardesses does not always precede a hassle-free trip to *Kantor Imigrasi*.

The problems begin before I even enter the building. After walking to the Indonesian Consulate in the boiling heat, the security guard informs me that I am not dressed for the occasion. You may not enter an Indonesian consulate or immigration office wearing shorts, a rule that I knew, but had carelessly forgotten. I whine to the young armed man that I do not have time to walk all the way to my friend's apartment and back, and I do not have the money for a taxi. He walks into the office and returns with a size "S" pair of navy blue, paper thin polyester pants. He gives me a look that says this is my only other option. The pants do not even make it up around my butt, even with my recent diet and all the walking knocking me down to my lowest weight since high school. They do at least cover my legs, which makes me decent enough to enter. I take very small steps into the office.

Once inside I take a ticket and wait to be called. I sit down on one of the maroon colored seats and repeat the name "Dr. Mudaffar Sjah, BcHk" over and over again. "Mud-af-far-Sjah-BcHk ...Mud-af-far-Sjah-BcHk." Dr. Mudaffar Sjah is the deceased former Sultan of Ternate, father of the current Sultan and grandfather of a good friend I made on my first trip to Indonesia, Prince Bhayu. Bhayu kindly offered to assist me in obtaining a six month cultural visa, which I am hoping will free me from having to step inside of another *kantor imigrasi*. In Bhayu's letter of recommendation he explains that Ternate's royal family is sponsoring me because I am writing a biography on the late Dr.

Mudaffar Sjah, BcHk. I try to make sure that I can at least pronounce the name of this man I am supposed to be writing a book about before my number is called. I realize that I do not even have a clue what the "BcHk" after his name stands for.

"7033" is called, and I walk like an old man with hemorrhoids up to the counter. A grim looking official behind the counter flips through my papers as I stand straight at attention. He asks me who my sponsor is and I tell him that my friend, the Prince of Ternate, is sponsoring me. He does not look impressed. He glances up at me a couple times and seems to be wondering how the late Sultan of Ternate would feel if he knew that a red-faced *bule* without a decent pair of pants was writing his biography. He grows more irritated as he reads. He says there is no way I am getting a six month visa. He says "if" they approve my visa it will be for sixty days and then I can conveniently renew it every 30 days at the nearest *kantor imigrasi.*

When arriving at Kuala Lumpur's airport, travelers from all countries grab a concise entry form, fill it out, move through a brisk line and without paying any fee, get a 90-day visa on arrival stamped to their passport. The first sight morning travelers to Padang see is one long line leading to a closed booth where an immigration official will make sure that you paid your 250,000 ($25) for your 30-day visa. If you arrive on an early flight you may have to wait until that immigration officer wakes up and gets to work.

An American friend of mine arriving at Jakarta's airport in 2008 was scolded for not having six months left on his passport before it expired. Although he had a return flight departing in two weeks, he was told that it was impossible for him to enter the country. After being taken to a private room, walked to an ATM to pull out two million rupiah ($200) for a "tip" and then back to the private room, the official finally put a stamp on his passport. I wonder if these immigration officials, the first face foreigners see, realize what a bad name they give to a country filled with so many honest, trustworthy people. And can they see that the reason Malaysia's tourism is growing is not just because they stole Indonesia's *rendang*?

The immigration officer hands my forms back to me along with one other form that needs to be autographed by my friend, the Prince of Ternate. Although Prince Bhayu is presently well over a thousand miles away on the island of Ambon, the next morning I head back to the consulate's *kantor imigrasi* with the form complete, by way of a magic trick I will not explain here.

I shake a leg trying to get the security guard to take note of my borrowed, starched, black suit pants, but he just waves me through. I repeat the words "Dr. Mudaffar Sjah, BcHk" to myself a few times and then curse myself for not looking up what the "BcHk" means. The same immigration official collects my papers and tells me to come back tomorrow.

The next day, wearing the same borrowed suit pants, I am handed a 60-day renewable cultural visa. I immediately walk toward an Air Asia office to book my flight to Jakarta. I never even had to pronounce Dr. Mudaffar Sjah's name.

***

Before we cross over to Java, I would like to go back in time, before my quarter-life crisis breakdown on the bus ride to Siantar, and give Aceh and Toba their fair due in my story.

3

ACEH

At 8:00 AM on my first morning in Aceh (pronounced aa-che) I awoke to the sound of Norman and four of his friends knocking on my hotel door. I had arrived after midnight and hastily went online to send a couch request. I opened a profile with Couch Surfing a couple years earlier, but had never actually stayed with or hosted another member. You can register with Couch Surfing just by opening a profile and providing some information on couchsurfing.com. You then have access to view other member's profiles and contact them. At the time of my trip, Couch Surfing had over 3.6 million members in 250 countries.

If you are passing through a town you can contact couch surfers there to meet you, show you around their town or even request a place to sleep. While less than 1% of the world's couch surfers call Indonesia home, those Indonesians who do join are proactive members seeking out guests in their town and offering couches, tours and travel advice. I told Norman where I was staying and sure enough, as if it was his job to play the gracious ambassador, Norman was there already to introduce me to his friends, give me a tour of Banda Aceh and save me the costs of a hotel for as long as I planned to stay in his city.

After the introductions, I hopped on the back of Norman's motorbike. All across Indonesia motorbikes are the most common form of transportation. These bikes are either automatic or four-speed manual and can usually get up to about 40 mph on an open road. *Ojeks*, basically taxi motorbikes, can be found in just about every city and town. With few exceptions, you can get from any part of a town to another by *ojek* for 5,000-20,000 rupiah ($0.50-$2.00).

Our first stop was a small gathering of military officials. Norman's political skills were immediately apparent. He walked through the crowd greeting officials, briefly summarizing what his program *Pray from Aceh* is doing. We were all wearing bright red *Pray from Aceh* t-shirts. Norman and his friends were wearing jeans even though the sun was blazing and the temperature was hovering at 90 degrees.

A born leader and fluent English speaker, on his way to finishing medical school, Norman was an invaluable asset to the 2004 Boxing Day tsunami recovery effort. Just 22 years old at the time, Norman treated patients, translated complex medical jargon, and guided international medical teams around an area that was already a turbulent place to be before the sixty foot waves came. Norman worked day and night for months on end. He worked so much he claims he never even had a minute to actually let the emotion of what was happening settle in. In mid-2005, as doctors became less instrumental to the recovery efforts, Norman made a commitment to stay connected with the rebuilding of his hometown.

The *Al Kahfi Foundation* is a youth community center that Norman founded with the help of friends. The center runs a number of programs that include raising money to help orphans pay tuition fees, providing free English lessons to teenagers and simply standing as a haven where young people can come to support one another. The community center, which is one large room, holds thousands of books, most of which Norman persuaded NGO workers to donate.

Pray from Aceh, the latest initiative of the *Al Kahfi Foundation,* revolves around the tsunami that hit Sentai, Japan. Norman had been encouraging Acehnese to go on his website to write their condolences and offer words of encouragement. Friends of Norman take these letters, translate them into Japanese and post them where they can be read by those suffering from the devastation of a natural disaster the Acehnese understand all too well.

Norman explained, "Japan is a rich country. Trying to collect money in Indonesia to send to Japan would be difficult and most likely not make much of an impact. This initiative allows us to connect with Japanese who are suffering. When we suffered after the tsunami, people from all over the world opened their wallets and hearts to us. We will never forget that, and when another part of the world suffers, we want them to know that we feel their pain."

***

Later that afternoon I went to a well-frequented café in the center of Banda Aceh with Norman and his friend, Hijrah. I quickly learned that hanging out at coffee shops is a favorite pastime of the Acehnese. Glancing around, it was hard to tell which tables were occupied with business and which were hosting less serious matters. I ordered a *kopi susu* and was quickly woken up by the drug-like dose of coffee and sugar.

A couple young women wearing *jilbabs* approached our table. Norman and Hijrah had a business meeting scheduled. I excused myself and went to another table to check emails on my iPad. While many parts of Indonesia remain in the Stone Age when it comes to providing even moderately acceptable internet services, the rush of NGOs that established themselves here in the wake of the tsunami have managed to make Aceh one of the speediest and most accessible Wi-Fi cities in Southeast Asia.

In between rummaging through emails, I glanced back over to watch Norman and Hijrah getting to work. They were trying to sell a trip to Mecca to these two young girls and two older women that joined the table.

They work for a company called *Arminareka Perdana*. The job is simple. They make contacts with as many people as possible and sell them an all-inclusive packaged trip to Mecca. The total cost of the trip is US$1,650 with a $250 deposit. Norman and Hijrah are rewarded with a $150 commission for each person they sign up. Their clients have wide leeway regarding when they actually take the trip with some taking years to pay off the balance. Once they make that deposit they will have put themselves on track to fulfill one of the main expectations of their religion. A trip to Mecca is one of the five pillars of Islam along with belief in one God, praying five times a day, giving to the poor and fasting during the month of Ramadan.

The trip to Mecca is expected if one has the means to travel. Indonesia is home to over 200 million Muslims. However, its location 4,000 miles from the Saudi Arabian Holy Land and a national yearly per capita income of that exact amount, $1,650, prevent the vast majority of Indonesians from stepping foot in Mecca. A strong selling point for Norman and Hijrah is that while a $1,650 trip may seem unrealistic, a $250 deposit and a gradual payment system can make this religious obligation attainable. Completing the trip to Mecca is a great honor for any Muslim. Men will often wear a plain white prayer cap for the rest of their lives to memorialize their achievement.

About an hour later the table was filled with smiles and handshakes. The four women, all wearing different bright colored *jilbabs*, had put a deposit down on checking off one of their requirements for life everlasting. Norman and Hijrah had secured two more pilgrims each. In an hour's worth of work sipping *kopi* and chatting, these two men in their late-20s each earned more than a month's salary of the average professor at my former university.

It was interesting to watch Norman and Hijrah during my time in Aceh. They would meet quite early most mornings over *kopi* to discuss their various money-making and altruistic ventures for the day. Norman spends much of his day at his community center hanging out with young locals. Hijrah runs his own clothing store that sells traditional Achenese knives and t-shirts promoting Aceh, particularly Sabang, which is famous for being the city closest to the country's western tip. All Indonesians are familiar with Sabang from the line of a nationalist song, often sung by young school children wearing their grade-color-coded uniforms, "Sabang ke Marauke." (Closest American translation: Lee Greenwood singing *"From New York to LA."*)

Norman and Hijrah in many ways emulate the very characteristics of Aceh, fiercely proud of their homeland and more or less detached from their country. Their eyes are always looking out from this archipelago for new ideas, business ventures and ways to connect and learn from other cultures. Locals like to claim that even the name Aceh is an acronym for the people who came from other places and embraced it: A – Arab; C – Chinese; E – European; H – Hindu.

Norman's features give off a hint of Chinese, while Hijrah could claim a mix of Hindu and Arab blood. Unlike many of the young people I have met in other parts of Indonesia, these two men are not looking to secure government jobs with rich benefits. They are searching for their own way. While it can be almost impossible to find an Indonesian Muslim willing to express a single critical opinion of their religion, Hijrah openly criticizes the wisdom of his province banning movie theaters and Norman praises the more critical study of Islam in places he has visited like southern Spain.

While Banda Aceh may not possess a bouncing nightlife, a big compensation is that you can hang out and drink *kopi susu* in coffee shops all night. That is exactly what we did. I met more of Norman's friends. I spent much of the night discussing politics with a 23-year-old, insightful part-time college professor. Ali, who had recently earned a degree in Egypt, had a fierce sternness in his look that did not fit his boyish features. He preached to me the ills of America's involvement in Libya and asked questions about "the poor in America," a rare topic of interest for your average Indonesian. I imagine that just as the Soviets did during the Cold War, Ali's professors have been teaching him to question the world's lone superpower and take note that many Americans are not fed an equal slice of the American dream. Then he quickly turns the subject to the problems of Aceh: not enough well-paying jobs, rampant cronyism involved in achieving those jobs, too much interference from Jakarta and worst of all, "No one here gets up to do anything. No do! Just sit in coffee shop and Talk! Talk! Talk!" I could not help but smile. Ali's last complaint perfectly summed up what I liked so much about Aceh.

***

Hijrah offered to take me on a trip to Sabang, so I could officially begin my trip on Indonesia's most geographically western island. On the 90-minute ferry ride, I sat next to a retired civil servant wearing a traditional black Muslim prayer cap. He told me about his grandfather, an Afghan merchant who fell in love with a local woman and never bothered to get back on the ship. He also had a son who earned a degree at the University of Indiana. I asked him if he has any desire to see the states for himself some day.

"Not really. But if the mess in Afghanistan cleans up it would be a dream come true to see my grandfather's country."

After docking at the city of Sabang, Hijrah drove me on the back of his motorbike to Kilometer Zero, a monument on the western tip of *Pulau* Weh that also marks the western tip of Indonesia's archipelago. The road there winds around a cliff dropping to the shore. There are palm trees lining the quiet road, many filled with coconuts and some watchful monkeys. The monument is a three-storied circular structure. The floors are cracked white tiles and the banisters are filled with engravings of names of people who have passed

92

through. There were two local teenage couples on a bench nearby. One of the teenagers had to get up and swing a stick at the aggressive monkeys looking for something to take. It was hard to tell whether the monkeys were being motivated by survival instincts or just looking for a laugh.

The monument is uncared for and surely seldom visited. Not many people care so much about reaching the western tip of Indonesia, and even less would bother to make the 3,253 mile (5,236 km) trip across the country that I was setting out on. Looking West at the Indian Ocean, you could imagine all the different groups of people that came to Indonesia, to trade, fight, rule, steal, convert, learn, teach, or travel. So many of them came straight to Aceh. It is a testament to their land how many people from so many different cultures decided not to just take their goods, wives or cultural lessons back to their own country, but to remain here and allow their descendants to be called Acehnese.

From Kilometer Zero we drove down to *Pantai* Gapong. On the way we passed a giant billboard, *"Lindungilah dari HIV/AIDS"* (Protection from HIV/AIDS) with a giant picture of Aceh's largest mosque, which appears to be offering not only eternal life in paradise, but also an STD-free life here on earth. A couple of small boats were waiting for a group of western tourists to sail out and dive *Pulau* Weh's world-renowned reefs. Hijrah and I sat down next to a group of Asians from different countries that seemed to be having a relaxed business meeting. Hijrah informed me that in a minute he would introduce me to the vice-mayor of Sabang. I never know who I am going to meet on this trip, and I realized I need to have my questions ready. Deputy Mayor Islamuddin (just one name) looks just slightly older than myself. Wearing jeans and a golf shirt, he had a very sincere yet relaxed manner about him. Although Islamuddin claimed his English is poor, we are able to speak for about twenty minutes with little trouble.

Islamuddin grew up on the mainland of Aceh. As an undergraduate he became involved with a student organization that played its role in ending the reign of another guy with one name, Suharto. A fellow member of his organization is the current mayor, who was studying in Egypt when Suharto was forced to resign in May of 1998. Islamuddin was just one of tens of thousands of students across the archipelago organizing rallies, making posters, encouraging underclassmen to get involved, splashing the waters so that the wave could be formed that would eventually free his country from the rule of one of the 20th century's most brutal dictatorships.

Just two months earlier, Egypt's oppressive government was overthrown in a historic revolution led by young Egyptians using Twitter and Facebook. Chances are a decade from now those idealistic students will be taking leading roles in their country's future just like Islamuddin and Mayor Munawar Liza Zainal. Like thousands of Indonesians, the mayor went to Egypt not only for an education, but to open his mind to foreign ideas.

Vice-Mayor Islamuddin also had a chance to go overseas. After finishing college he was invited to attend a four day cultural conference in Washington DC. In November 2001, he flew to the states with plans to backpack around America for two months and see what this country, which he had only experienced through Hollywood movies, had to offer. "It was an exciting time. I had always wanted to see America."

At the airport in Detroit he was stopped by immigration officials, interrogated for four hours and eventually had his three-month visa chopped down to four days. He had just enough time to attend his conference, walk around the Washington Mall and get back on a cross continental plane, possibly losing his only chance to travel the nation that prides itself as a beacon of freedom.

As the world's largest Muslim country, Indonesia is considered a battleground of ideas, a democracy that allows caning and bikinis, sometimes, as in Aceh, in the same province. For every Starbucks that pops up in a major city, a remote village responds by opening a radical Islamic school funded by Middle Eastern oil. For every pirated Hollywood DVD that arrives in the country there is a headscarf being sown in Central Java.

Those who leave Indonesia and return often become the country's strongest catalysts for change. I did not have to travel very far from Kilometer Zero to find a missed opportunity for the United States.

***

On a quiet Tuesday morning back on the mainland of Sumatra, Norman drove me out to Ulee Lheue, a port town that was literally washed away with the tsunami. Later that day he showed me the "Tsunami Ship," a 2,600 ton ship that leveled everything in its path before flattening and docking atop the rubble of a row of houses almost two miles inland. A smiling old man led me up to the top of that ship, and we looked out all the way to the ocean as he informed me that his house is buried under the ship. But before that strange journey in natural disaster tourism, we went to meet someone who could teach me about GAM, *Gerakan Aceh Merdeka* (Free Aceh Movement). Aceh's long struggle for independence was the issue on everyone's lips before the city of Banda Aceh lost more than half its population.

Aceh's history is one full of pride and resistance. Most resource-filled areas of the archipelago fell under Dutch control as soon as those resources were discovered. The Dutch were not able to establish their authority over Aceh until a brutal 30-year war ended in 1903. (An ironic glance back through history shows that during the Netherland's Eighty Year War (1568-1648) for independence from Spain, Aceh was the first nation to recognize the sovereignty of the Netherlands). While Aceh did support the Indonesian Revolution, and in the initial years after World War II, a unified Indonesian nation, by 1953 Aceh had grown disillusioned with their national government and was prepared to take up arms against their new enemies in Jakarta. With a permanent military presence in Aceh, the situation would range from high tension to all-out war over the next half century.

A high point in the conflict followed Mobil's 1971 discovery of natural gas reserves which would create and fuel the largest natural gas plant in the world, eventually accounting for 30% of Indonesia's oil and gas exports. The Acehnese believed these profits were only being invested in Java. It is a common perception in many parts of Indonesia that the profits from each region's resources disproportionately benefit the island of Java. The roads I traveled through in Sumatra over two months can be counted as one example. I spent 85 hours in buses and vans going over terrain that at times resembled a monster truck derby course while in Java a comfortable train connects the west and east sides of the island.

Norman had informed me that I would interview Iskandar, a former GAM soldier. Iskandar showed up, but said very little and acted more like a bodyguard to a surprise guest, Mohammad Dahlan, who with a sturdy build and a thick beard is a well-known spokesman and leader of GAM's revolution. Dahlan joined GAM in its early stages while he was still in high school. He attended university in Jakarta and later became a journalist, often stretching the limits of how

97

much the government and President Suharto could be criticized. In 1988 a friend of his in intelligence tipped him off that he had crossed the line and was about to be blacklisted. Dahlan fled to Australia. Today he splits his time between Australia and Aceh and has remained a leading public figure in GAM, which has become a recognized political party in Aceh.

In 1976 Hasan di Tiro, who studied in New York City and was the descendant of a famous Acehnese war hero, officially formed GAM. Fueled by Jakarta's indifference to the needs of Acehnese and frustrated with prior Acehnese revolts, which seemed more concerned with spreading a stricter form of Islam throughout the archipelago, di Tiro led his revolt from a secret outpost deep in the hills. Armed with his typewriter, and under the protection of his loyal followers di Tiro spent much of his time writing his arguments for the necessity of an Acehnese nation. In 1977, after being shot in the leg during an intense manhunt, Hasan di Tiro fled Aceh. He would not return to Indonesian soil for more than 30 years. His arrival in 2008 came three years after he helped broker a peace treaty with the Indonesian government granting autonomy with special privileges, but not independence for Aceh.

Mohammad Dahlann spoke of Hasan di Tiro with as much admiration as Tibetans speaking about the Dali Lama. He rattled off the names of de Tiro biographies that I must read and shows me pictures of the two of them just prior to di Tiro's death in 2010. But

Dahlan does not believe the 2005 peace treaty was a fair agreement. "Aceh was under too much pressure to sign because we needed aid to flow freely through the province. This treaty needed years to work out the details, not a couple of months." The treaty called for GAM to disarm its roughly 3,000 fighters and surrender to Jakarta control of finances, defense and foreign policy. In return Jakarta allowed Aceh to use its regional flag, limited the number and movement of government troops in Aceh, allowed for the establishment of a court to expose human rights abuses and mandated that 70% of the region's natural resources would stay in Aceh.

I asked Dahlan if he believes that 70% of the region's resources have stayed in Aceh. "We do not have any say in monitoring this so how can we know? But I don't think so."

Finally I asked Dahlan what he wants me to tell Americans about Aceh. "Help Aceh to become free. Tell American businessmen to invest directly into Aceh, not through Jakarta. Jakarta only wants Aceh's resources and land. They do not care about the Acehnese. Tell them Aceh is not Indonesia." When asked to describe the state of GAM today, Dahlan responded, "Right now, we are sleeping."

Later that evening as I walked around the Baiturrahman Mosque downtown I wondered, with all of the resentment still fueling Acehnese, how long this hibernation would last? I stopped to take a photo of

Aceh's largest mosque, an impeccably white structure under three coal black domes. I stopped at a distance just in front of a pole holding the Indonesian national flag, wanting to get a picture of the flag with the mosque behind it. After about ten minutes I realized that even the Acehnese wind did not want to see this flag flown.

***

It is hard to imagine a place suddenly losing 170,000 of its people, almost the entire population of my hometown of Yonkers, New York. It is difficult to picture a half a million people becoming homeless overnight, and it is impossible to comprehend the pain that must have engulfed this area. Every day I was in Aceh I met someone in their twenties or younger who had lost one or both parents.

One night as I am drinking *kopi* and swapping stories with Norman late into the night, he opens up about how that day affected him. Norman was eating breakfast and watching cartoons when he felt the earthquake on December 26, 2004. His mother was washing clothes. She grabbed some important papers and they ran to a nearby hill. Minutes later their house was washed away with the tsunami.

When the water receded Norman ran down the hill and began to conduct CPR on victims. "I remember a man crying with his young daughter lying limp in his arms, begging me to help. I just stared. I couldn't find the words to tell him she was dead." The aftershocks continued to shake the land throughout the afternoon.

Each earthquake, a fierce warning that another tsunami could be minutes away. Each time Norman was forced to stop CPR or attending to a victim's wounds and sprint back up the hill. "I didn't want to leave them, but the old people would scream, 'Go! Leave us! Get out of here!' " And Norman would run, not knowing if he would ever see any of their faces again.

The recovery was no less dramatic for Norman and the surviving Acehnese. Months later the body of one of Norman's best friends, who was also his mentor in medical school, was found in a tree. In all of the destruction and chaos, almost six months passed before all five of Norman's sisters were accounted for. They all survived, but most of his extended family did not. Dozens of his aunts, uncles and cousins remain unaccounted for.

It was not until almost one full year later that the devastation set in for Norman. It was *Idul Fitri*, the most important Muslim holiday of the year when Achenese cook feasts and visit family throughout the day, wishing each other happiness and prosperity in the year to come. "Ever since I was a kid that day was the happiest day of the year. It was the end of the fasting month, and I would see my cousins and we would eat every last bite of food Mom cooked for us. That *Idul Fitri* was so quiet with just a few guests stopping in. That night I sat at our kitchen table staring at all of that food. That was when it finally sunk in for me. They're not coming back."

Baiturrahman Grand Mosque, Aceh

Aceh

4

Lake Toba

I was sitting in the open air lounge of *Bagus* (Good) Bay Guesthouse when Budi walked in. In his mid-20s, Budi speaks English well and does not try too hard with catch phrases many of his peers think foreigners love hearing like "dude," "mate" and "bro." I knew exactly why Budi wandered in. It was not to try the pizza. Budi is one of hundreds of young people without a job scattered across Indonesia's tourist towns looking for a foreigner to spend the day with and make a few dollars off. Budi is not a con artist or a shyster, but like all Indonesians who work the tourist circuits, he is not quite as innocent as he seems.

These freelancing all-around tour guides love to make it seem like they discovered you by chance, a tryst arranged by the heavens. They enter your trip out of the blue to rescue you from feeling like a tourist. Now you are an explorer who has a local friend to take you around the sites and restaurants, introducing you to other interesting locals who tell their stories freely, giving you an insider's peak into the lives of these people and providing you with a story to tell your friends back home as well as a Facebook friend who will always remember to write on your wall every birthday. And all you have to do is pick up the bill at each restaurant and sometimes give them a few bucks for taking you around, which they are not shy about telling you is "cheap for you."

Maybe I am being slightly cynical towards these nice young people who are really just trying to take a rare opportunity to make money, improve their English, learn about the outside world and enjoy a day. Plus they are very often helpful with arranging travel, helping you find whatever you need, as well as being trustworthy. But after almost four years in Asia, I can not help but be turned off any time I meet someone with hidden motives.

I reflect back on my first trip to Toba, three years earlier, during Chinese New Year, 2008. It was my first real backpacking experience and Samosir Island, located inside of and taking up most of Lake Toba, was the first stop. I was travelling with Ed, a friend who taught at the same international school. After arriving on the last ferry, Ed and I dropped our luggage off at *Bagus* Bay, checked the internet to learn that our Giants had just beaten the undefeated Patriots in one of the biggest Super Bowl upsets ever, and started walking toward the bar to celebrate.

It was a dark night, and we were getting a little tired of leaning off the road and into the bushes every time a motorbike drove by, blinding us. Then these two guys pulled their bikes off the road and one yelled in broken English, "Party down road . . . many girls . . . want to go?" We looked at each other and using our good judgment and the knowledge that we were twice the size of them hopped on the backs of their bikes. They delivered on their promise, and for the next few days we hung out with them routinely, going to young local's houses and bars. We learned after the third round at the first bar how it worked. They handled all the driving and the introductions and we handled the tab. I enjoyed it. I learned a lot from the people we met and it felt good to know I always had a ride home. I did not get turned off until a few nights later when they took me to a fancier sit-down restaurant where we met a group of their friends and drank some *Bintangs*. When the overpriced bill came, everyone looked at me. On other occasions I at least had the freedom to go to the bar, order the amount of drinks I chose and then pick a table and share them with whom I chose. I decided that would be the last time I played the *bule* with the generous wallet.

Over the next few days I lightened up a good bit toward Bumi. I watched him wandering around in the mornings, greeting tourists, trying to figure how to make a buck. He was awkward at first, not knowing whether to start with one of the more typical lines like, "Where are you from?" or something that fits the individual more like, "Blond-haired women are the most beautiful. I wish Asia had more of them."

Most days he would get lucky, and at dinner I could overhear in an Australian or British accent, "What a nice boy that Bumi was? We sure got our money's worth out of that tour!" Quite often Bumi would find a woman travelling alone and get even luckier, showing up the following morning with bloodshot eyes, and a good story for his friends. Every day Bumi lives in a strange world where he must compete with many of his own people for the attention and money of a handful of tourists.

There used to be a lot more tourists on Samosir Island. Ask almost anyone selling t-shirts, sarongs or wood carvings why business has slowed in the last ten years and you will get a similiar answer, "Because of the terrorists." "Because Indonesia has too many Muslims."

The Batak region is one of the few predominantly Christian areas of the country. Apparently tourism on the island took a steep drop after the psychological aftershocks of 9/11 reverberated around the world. Attacks on Indonesian soil, mainly attributed to Jemaah Islamiah (JI), a terrorist group with ties to Al Qaeda, made matters even worse. JI focused its terror on two areas, Bali, an island which attracts more tourists than the entire rest of the country combined, and Jakarta, the capital city that attracts almost every person doing business in Indonesia. JI is suspected of being responsible for the bombings of the Australian embassy in 2004, two tourist areas of Bali in 2005, Jakarta's JW Marriott hotel in 2003, and in 2009 simultaneous bombings at the same JW Marriot and a Ritz-Carlton, where the Manchester United football team was due to check in the following day. In JI's deadliest attack on Indonesian soil, a nightclub in Bali was bombed in 2002 killing over 200 people, mostly Australian tourists. Many Western travelers were naturally keen to cross the world's largest Muslim country off their vacation list. Places like Lake Toba, whose survival relies primarily on tourist dollars, were hit hardest.

***

Tuk-Tuk is the section of Samosir Island where tourists stay. A peninsula with most of the island's hotels, restaurants, and souvenir shops filled with Batak wooden carvings and sarongs on one road that hugs the lake. There are about a dozen places with 200-500 books for sale or rent with Gokohn's Book Store offering possibly the best selection in Sumatra. To put that into perspective, Padang, a city of almost one million people, has two bookstores with a total of about twenty English books, and you can not find a single one written in the last 100 years.

Most of the stores and restaurants are empty at any given time. The guesthouses seem content if one or two of their rooms are filled. Often I would walk into a restaurant only to be greeted by the owner's children who need to run up the block to snatch Mom from her friend's house. There is a wide variety of foods available from Indonesian rice dishes to hamburgers to hallucinogenic mushroom pizza. One night in search of dinner, I walked into Today's Cafe, wondering if they are open. The motto on their menu explained it for me, "Always Open If Not Close." They are very creative with their dishes. One dish takes the sauce from *rendang* and mixes it with baked potatoes.

The owners, Julietti and Asima, were very polite about letting me enjoy my meal, and then joining me when I finished. They are in their early 30s and unmarried, which they say in Batak culture is considered strange. Asima said that her seven brothers are always trying to set her up with someone and that often these men start speaking of marriage on the first few dates. "I want to wait until I find the right person. Not just marry to marry." It is actually not uncommon to hear an Indonesian man who becomes financially stable and established in his career say, "I think I will marry this year." This would not sound so strange if he already had a girlfriend.

I mentioned to Julietta and Asima that I sell pearl and stone jewelry. They asked to have a look and before I knew it I was spending most of the next few days dropping in on Batak women to fill their jewelry needs. The excursion helped me fund most of my time in Toba, but did not come without its headaches. Bataks are some of the toughest bargainers I have come across. Telling them that every piece is already heavily discounted off my New York prices did not faze them. And right when I thought the deal had been made I was always hit with a smilingly, "Now what are you going to throw in for free?"

Bataks are notorious for being some of the most jealous, provincial people in the region, and I began to see where the stereotype comes from. My once quiet, peaceful walks around the lake were turned into trials where I was accosted and accused of giving Ati or Vionna or Alyssa a better deal. I put up my best defense.

"The necklace I sold Ati is a dime a dozen, but what you picked out is a one of a kind piece. I could search a hundred years and never find anything like it." Then before I can walk another five minutes I see Ati waiting outside her hotel with her eyes squinted and her cell phone in her hand.

***

Just over three years ago on my first trip to Toba my friend Ed and I stopped at a traditional blanket weaving colony during a ride around the island. About half a dozen women worked outside, meticulously weaving blankets by hand. The families of these women all lived on the same dirt road lined with a row of traditional Batak houses. Their many children of all ages played in the open area in between the houses. Instead of dolls, young girls carried their baby siblings around, and the chickens, dogs and boars mixed freely with the children. We took a lot of pictures that day, and Ed promised to print out the pictures and mail them to these families. Ed, not being one to break a promise, never mailed the pictures, but instead handed over the photos and responsibility to me. So three years and 2 months later, after bartering a pearl bracelet for a motorbike rental, I set out with six of Ed's 8x10s and a few of my own 3x5s to find Lumbansuhisuhi village.

Driving around Samosir Island is intoxicating. Every view of lush Batak land reaching down to the water is a portrait. Every turn offers a majestic glimpse into another time. Everything about Toba seems like something taken out of a fairy tale. And if you ask any Batak to tell you the history of their people, that is exactly what it sounds like.

Si Raja Batak, the Father of all Bataks, is believed to have been a child born of the gods on *Bukit* Pusuk on the western edge of Samosir Island. Si Raja Batak had two sons, and from these two sons and their two wives (no mention in the story of where the wives originated from) more sons were born with each becoming the first ancestor of a *Marga* (Batak family line). Today you may meet someone who calls him/herself Hutasoit 22 (22nd generation) or Lontung 31 (31st generation). One of my Batak friends living in Bali hates meeting other Bataks because it is expected that the first thing two Bataks must do when meeting is trace their lineage until they figure out how they are related. Apparently this can take a long time. One reason this is important is because if two Bataks are found to be part of the same family line, marrying would be considered incestuous.

It is not like a *marga* and generation number are just suffixes following Batak names. As I once listened to a Batak friend reminisce about his days working as a hotel manager. "One of my receptionists was constantly coming to work late. Finally I told him I had to write him up for an infraction. He just stared at me for a long time and responded, 'I am an older generation than you, and my great ancestor, grandson of Si Raja Batak, was older than your great ancestor. And you think you can write me up!'"

As I drove along on my Honda Vario motorbike around this enchanted island, the lake dropped down to my right side, at times a dark royal blue, other times it seemed to blend in with the sky. To my left, the land rose for rice paddies, and grazing goats. The healthy green land is showered with crosses, atop churches, graves, and other random structures. I passed one cross made of tiles that must have reached fifty feet high. The cemeteries are filled with mini Batak houses underneath large wooden crosses that look like holy dog houses.

The Bataks were not converted until the late 1800s when Dutch, English and German missionaries raced to save these mountain people (Lake Toba is almost 3,000 feet above sea level) after hearing stories of cannibalism, which was practiced, at least in war and as a punishment for criminals. I wonder if the Batak people hang these crosses out of pride in their religion, as much as they do to show that they are an exception in Indonesia. After so many generations of wars with their Muslim neighbors to the north, the Bataks seem to celebrate everything not Muslim. Some of their best known dishes include pork. Dogs are familiar pets at guesthouses, strutting with pride and barking at you without that timid, defeated demeanor dogs have in Muslim areas of the country. Bataks are not shy about snatching up Western tourists to be their husbands, wives or lovers. They are keen to join in on the drinking festivities, especially when someone mixes up a batch of *tuak*, a bitter palm wine made from fermented rice, yeast and sugar. To me, the Bataks would seem more at home with the Irish or Mexicans than with any of their fellow countrymen.

With the strong presence of Islam for hundreds of years in many places, Christianity made little headway into most parts of Indonesia, especially in Java. Where European missionaries did find some luck was in the remote areas that still practiced animist beliefs. The largest pockets of Christianity grew in Papua, Sulawesi, Ambon, parts of Kalimantan and here in the Batak highlands.

Bataks, whose skin is normally a much darker brown than those of Sumatra's other ethnic groups, are historically believed to be descendants of the areas later recognized as northern Burma and Siam (that is of course if you do not believe in Si Raja Batak's descent from heaven). While the Bataks did have settlements along the coast that traded with other parts of the Indies and Southeast Asia, the majority of the population rested in these hard to reach highlands. Even today, travelers landing at Medan's airport must take a four and a half hour ride in a Toyota Kijang to reach Lake Toba.

After stopping numerous times and asking for Lumbansuhisuhi, I ended up driving down a dirt road I recognized. As one would expect the area had not changed. An old woman greeted me chewing her betel nut, a blood red fruit that when chewed offers a slight-euphoric buzz. It is commonly chewed by old women in remote parts of Indonesia and leaves a harsh stain in one's mouth. Since it is spit out routinely it leaves dark red puddles, making it look like someone nearby is bleeding to death.

The Batak houses are made of wood and traditionally were built without using a single nail. They often took as long as five years to build. The roofs are palm thatched, which make them easily susceptible to fires. The houses have three floors. The top floor is used as an attic usually storing no more than a few family heirlooms. The middle floor is where everyone else sleeps, the children on the floor, and the husband and wife on a wooden board that does not look much more comfortable than the floor. The ground floor is where the farm animals sleep. The animals can be seen through a plate-sized hole in the second floor, which the inhabitants use a toilet that sends its waste freefalling down to the animals' ground floor apartment.

There were children running around, shy at first, but eventually they came around and allowed me to take their photos. They laughed when they saw each other's pictures on my camera. I tried to recognize their faces from the pictures three years prior, but I could not make any out. I walked around, poking my head into houses, trying to remember which one Ed made his promise to.

I approached one of the houses with three women outside hard at work sewing blankets by hand. They immediately tried to persuade me to buy a blanket. *"Cantik selimut!"* (Beautiful blanket!) I figured I was at the right place so I took the pictures out of my bag. One of the old women saw herself in one of the pictures and started yelling. Before I knew it half the village was surrounding us and little kids' dirty hands were tugging away at their pictures. They managed to put more creases in the pictures in two minutes than I did hauling them around in my bag for years. They asked, *"untuk Saya?"* (for me?) Before the pictures all went their separate ways, I told the women that they are gifts, but that if any of the people in the pictures are here that I would like to take a picture of them holding it. The children posed for their pictures, some willingly, others very unwillingly. The adults all thanked me and asked me to pass on their thanks and wishes of good health to my friend, Ed.

I expected the adults to take the photos from their kid's grubby hands and put them somewhere safe, maybe in a scrapbook on the third floor or on a wall. They did not. Some of the kids rolled their picture in their hand. Others lost interest and dropped them on

114

the ground. The older women continued weaving their blankets and tried again to persuade me to buy one. "*Selimut!* Very cheap for you!" The children started chanting a word I did not recognize. I looked it up in my dictionary; "Candy." One of the women from the house next door looked at me surprisingly and said, "*Tidak ada manisan?*" (Don't have candy?) I confessed that no, I did not have candy. I could have spent $1 at the store up the road and bought enough candy to give the entire village a sugar rush, but instead I brought 8x10s and 3x5s through four countries and six Indonesian provinces without getting a single bend in them.

I remembered talking with Ed about how none of the families had pictures in their houses. We both came from families that valued photographs. I came from a home where my Mom rotated photos religiously around the house from her endless supply. We naively believed that photos would be the most cherished gift these families could receive. But just like the classic lessons from *The Ugly American* of diplomats whose idea of giving aide to a developing country is building a six lane highway through a village where no one owns a car, I realized that our assumptions of what people from the Third World need or want are often wrong. The children escorted my motorbike out of the village, and I left without a *selimut*.

***

That night at my guesthouse the owner, Mr. John, was joined by four of his fellow band members, all dressed in traditional Batak clothing and ready to rock out. With a slightly hunched-back, Mr. John spends his days wandering around, looking lost as his son manages the front office. It is almost startling to hear him speak English since it is not a skill many Indonesians his age have had the time or opportunity to pick up.

Mr. John preluded each song with a short explanation in English. Some of the songs were for weddings, some about secret loves between young people and others about growing old. All had a similar rhythm. There were six musicians; two keeping a steady beat on different drums, another playing a wooden flute, a younger man on the guitar, a rough looking guy in the back whacking the gongs and Mr. John in front played what must be the most traditional of instruments, a metal knife tapping against a green *Bintang* beer bottle. The music was purely instrumental except for when Mr. John routinely blasted out a battle cry sounding "Heeeeeeeeeeeeeey!"

I had one last gift from Ed to give that night. Seeing how interested Mr. John was in photography, Ed asked me to give his old Canon Powershot camera to the old man. During a break in the music I told Mr. John about Ed, and he quickly interrupted to say that he did not remember him. I did not expect him to. I handed him the camera. He smiled, said "thank you," shook my hand, asked me to thank Ed and walked back to his band. If you are the kind of person who loves to be showered with gratitude when giving a gift, Indonesia will surely disappoint you. I recall an Indonesian story in which a mother tells her son, "You have become like these foreigners; always saying thank you, but with no gratitude in your heart."

Mr. John continued his knife and bottle routine. When the traditional show ended, the younger, and in my opinion, more talented guys took over. Guitars, banjos and some of this earth's best hidden voices filled the air. They sang in Indonesian and Batak, but mostly in English. The Doors' *Light My Fire* and the closest rendition to Louie Armstrong's *What a Wonderful World* I have ever heard. They passed around their homemade *tuak,* or jungle juice as they call it, encouraging the European girls to drink up and sing along.

Late into the night I saw Mr. John, still awake and hiding in a corner, snapping pictures and smiling each time he saw his photography on the screen.

Lumbansuhisuhi Village, Lake Toba

Lumbansuhisuhi Village, Lake Toba

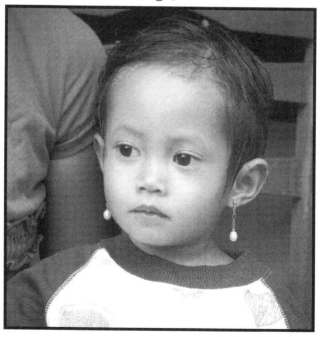

Lake Toba

5

Jakarta

I spend a couple nights at a hostel on *Jalan* Jaksa, Jakarta's *bule* street filled with drunken tourists and locals trying to get money off them. There are also more homosexuals and transvestites than any street I have seen in the country. It is a good base to see a few of the city's sights. I walk around the idle docks of Old Batavia (the city's name during the Dutch reign) and the streets of Menteng, where little Barry Obama and his friends flew kites. I walk by the last house he lived in, a one-story home with a red tiled roof squeezed in to *Jalan* Taman Amir Hamzah.

Ann Dunham relocated to Jakarta with her Indonesian husband and her six-year-old son in 1967. Unable to afford the international school, Obama's mother supplemented her son's education with lessons from a US correspondence course. The President fondly recalled, "Five days a week she came into my room at four in the morning, force-fed me breakfast and proceeded to teach me my English lessons for three hours before I left for school and she went to work."[12]

Just a couple blocks down the road is his old school with a small mirrored plaque stating that the 44th president of the United States studied there. His third grade teacher, *Bu* Fer, remembers a foretelling paper young Barry wrote which ended, *"Cita-cita saya adalah ingin jadi presiden. Saya suka jalan-jalan keliling Indonesia. Sudah Selasaaaaaaaaaai."* (Someday I want to be president. I love to visit all the places in Indonesia. Done. The Eeeeeeeeend.)[13]

Jakarta is known for its night life and not much else. My first night I find the Jaya Pub. There is a jazz band playing, a pool table and goofy stuff on the wall, similar to what you would expect to find at a TGI Friday's. It is mostly an older crowd with a few ex-pats scattered around. Running into other foreigners in a country like Indonesia can be a strange experience. People often leave the comforts of their own worlds in an attempt to experience the "Real Indonesia" or "Real (insert country)." The funny thing is they often get frustrated soon enough and find places like this that are the farthest thing from the "real" anything. But as much as we like our comforts like cushioned seats, cold beer and goofy stuff on the wall, running into other foreigners can be disarming. It forces the lone travelers to stop recording their self-scripted tale of a stranger in a strange land and realize that someone else has also left the luxury of the developed world and is intent on seeing more of the country than just *Jalan* Jaksa. Or as Joseph Conrad, sailing through the Indies over 100 years ago, more cynically described his fellow shipmates, "They loved short passages, good deck chairs, large native crews and the distinction of being white."[14]

Maybe I am feeling my own urge for distinction, or more likely I realize that a 43,000 rupiah ($4.30) bill for a small Heineken is not something I can keep up. Especially when last night after going through my finances I figured I would be fine if I just kept my total weekly expenses under 850,000 rupiah ($85) while making at least half that money back selling pearls and stones. After paying my tab, I wave down an *ojek* and take a twenty minute ride down to Block M. Riding the back of a motorbike at night might be the only way to beat the humidity of this city.

Block M is Jakarta's most popular area for bars and clubs, which I figure is a necessary stop on my cross-country tour. I have a beer in one bar while listening to an ex-pat who works for a foreign oil company tell me how lazy the Indonesians are and how it is impossible for them to get anything done unless he is constantly on their backs. He says the women work much harder than the men. He feels no urge personally to get back home, but only for the sake of his son. "I don't want him growing up in a country where he goes to school with the children of the wealthiest families and ends up thinking he is better than the locals. I also don't want to send him to their schools."

Before I can make my exit, an athletic looking local in a tight shirt challenges me to arm wrestle him. I know I should just politely refuse, but I have always been a better arm wrestler than my lean frame would suggest, and I can not remember the last time I competed in anything. I put him down three times before I leave the bar, feeling a little more confident, as his friends make fun of him.

I wander around outside hoping to find a small venue with live music. By some stroke of luck, I hear punk rock coming from a side street. There is a teenage band playing outside of a Circle K convenience store. The 7-Elevens back home purposely play classical music outside their stores to discourage teenagers from hanging out. I learn from the manager that Circle K's all around the country are inviting young bands to perform on their small patios. I am thrilled with the idea. I meet some band members that will be playing at another Circle K the following night. They are loaded with questions about America, and want to hear my whole life story. With good music and reasonably priced beer I am more than happy to play the worldly, old, foreign guy. I buy a sleeve of plastic cups and a couple big bottles of San Miguel, the only non-light beer you can find unless you like drinking Guinness out of a can. I pass the cups out to the musicians at my table. At first they refuse, wanting to make a point that they just want to talk and are not looking to take advantage of the *bule,* since they can not afford to return the favor. I tell them I appreciate that, and before long everyone has a drink in their hand, and we are all talking nostalgically about Hollywood, where not one of us has ever been.

They all wear jeans and t-shirts, and although they speak limited English most have no trouble singing their favorite songs in English. Budi, who has very white skin and long black hair, is from the Sulawesi islands. Northern Sulawesi, beginning with the Portuguese explorers and continuing through the Dutch, has seen more cross-breeding with Europeans than any other part of the country. Since Asians place the lightness of skin tone as one of the main factors when judging beauty, girls from this area are considered the most beautiful in the country. Rex is a drummer from Kalimantan. There are two brothers from *West Timor* (West East), a Batak and a Mandurese. Similar to Washington DC, no one seems to actually be from the capital city. A few offer me their emails in case I make my way through their hometowns.

Rex asks me if I know a way they can get to America. I ponder this over looking at these guys who probably do not have $20 dollars or two high school degrees among the group. I offer my two best ideas, "Keep playing music and hope you become famous or get a job on a cruise ship and jump ship in the States."

The next night I skip the bars completely and hang out with the guys at a different Circle K.

***

The events of the night of September 30, 1965 mark the most dramatic moment in Indonesia's political history. Like 9-11 in America, the night marked a point in time where all other events would then become historically known as "pre-" or "post-" and is shrouded with as much mystery and conspiracy as JFK's assassination.

Sukarno, who had led Indonesia since its Declaration of Independence twenty years earlier went to sleep in power that night. The next morning when he found the street to the State Palace blocked, he scurried to get all military forces under his direct command. He soon learned that General Suharto had already taken command, and that six of the military's top generals and one lieutenant were dead.

Two weeks later, Suharto had control over the three most important military posts. Two months later Suharto had full authority to determine who would be tried, prosecuted and preside as judges in the investigation and trial of the September 30th Movement. A March 1966 executive order transferred much of Sukarno's power to Suharto, and one year later Indonesia's parliament, under military control, elected Suharto president. On June 21, 1970 Sukarno died in his home. In his final years he was denied both medical care and visitors outside of his immediate family. The Father of Indonesia was not even granted his wish of being buried in Bogor, just south of Jakarta. Instead his body was taken to a remote village on the other side of Java.

September 30, 1965 was not a clear-cut coup d'état of one general taking power from a president. In the military-controlled media it was a portrayed as a failed coup orchestrated by the *PKI* (Indonesia's communist party). At the time, Indonesia's communist party was the second largest in the world. With more than three million members and ten million supporters, the communists were viewed as a threat to Indonesia's military, radical Islamists and especially to the world's Western powers. Although we may never know exactly who was behind the killings of September 30th, it soon became very obvious that the communists and alleged communists would be the ones to pay. In villages across Indonesia innocent men and women were pulled from their homes, tortured, murdered, thrown into ditches and rivers and soon enough forgotten about. While some estimates put the total number of killed in the aftermath at 2 million, historians agree that in the eighteen months following September 30, 1965 at least half a million were killed. The majority of murders were carried out by civilians as military and police forces stood by and watched. For many people, particularly public officials, there was an intense pressure to wash their hands of the communists and prove their loyalty to Suharto's New Order. Under Suharto's regime approximately 250,000 Indonesians served time as political prisoners.[15]

On another sunny Jakarta morning my friend Jenny and I ride a motorbike out to south side of the city to find *Lubang Buaja* (Crocodile Hole), a well where the bodies of those six generals and one lieutenant were dumped in the early morning hours of October 1, 1965. Driving a motorbike in Jakarta is much different from other parts of the country. There are many more motorbikes on the road and many more cars to drive around. In rush hour traffic, the long string of bikes snake around cars in constant succession.

I did not realize that the well happens to be on military grounds. I would have thought that whoever was responsible for those seven deaths would have at least found a less incriminating location to leave the evidence. Two soldiers at an entrance outpost stop us and ask us what our business is here. I tell them that I would like to see the well. They say that the well is closed today due to renovations. I wonder how much renovation can be done to a stone well that is only special because of the seven bodies that were once thrown into it. Jenny explains that I am writing a book about Indonesia, and that this is my only chance to see this historically significant spot. No chance. We ask if a "tip" to these hard working soldiers might make a difference. Still no chance. I have to settle for Googling pictures of the well.

For most Jakartanese, the only time they see *Lubang Buaya* is on a mandatory school trip in which they are fed the official government explanation that the evil communists were trying to take over their country, and that it was the courage of General Suharto and other members of the military that saved Indonesia.

The dream of millions that was Indonesia, that had endured colonialism, a WWII occupation and a war to achieve independence would be unequally distributed to the visions of two men, with just two names between them and two letters to differentiate them from each other for a combined 53 years. Sukarno's harshest criticisms came from acting in dictatorial fashion and playing the country's forces against one another. General Suharto made little effort to hide the fact that he was a dictator. The military had his back. For the country's political players, radical Islamists, journalists, separatist groups and anyone thinking about expressing an opposing view, they could just learn from the example he made of the communists.

Suharto ruled Indonesia for more than thirty years, longer than Mao Zedong ruled China. During his reign, infrastructure was improved, the economy grew, and Indonesia came to be regarded as a stable member of the world community. Also during this period, elections were rigged, political dissent was silenced, the media constrained and regional uprisings brutally repressed. Suharto is said to have built his own family fortune to an estimated 15-35 billion U.S. dollars during his presidency. Although he did not seem to spend much of it, living the final decade of his life unlavishly and in seclusion, praying five times a day at his home in the Menteng section of Jakarta.

Back at Crocodile Hole, Jenny and I are a little disappointed that we drove all the way out here and we can not even get a glimpse of this well where the seven bodies and an untold story were buried in 1965. We backtrack off the military grounds and hop off the bike to stretch our legs. After a short discussion we hop back on the motorbike, and I experience what it is like to drive in the mid-day heat from the south side to the east side of one of the world's most congested, polluted cities.

The *macet* (traffic) is congested, but not unbearable. After a lot of zipping around basically parked cars on the highway and a lot of Jenny yelling at me that I drive too slow, we finally arrive at our destination, the central quad of Trisakti University. I listen to a group of fashionably dressed co-eds of this well-to-do private school talking into their BlackBerrys. If *Lubang Buaya* is the ambiguous spot where the Suharto regime began in 1965, this quad is the equally ambiguous site where it ended.

By the spring of 1998, the Asian economic crisis had swept across Indonesia. The rupiah had fallen to more than a quarter of its value, food riots engulfed East Java and nine out of ten companies on Jakarta's stock exchange were found to be technically bankrupt.[16] In the midst of all this, Indonesia's parliament, in which appointments of 60% of its delegates were controlled by Suharto, unanimously reelected Suharto President for the seventh time.[17]

Here at Trisakti University and in other parts of the country, Indonesians were beginning to let their long silenced voices be heard. It was the killing of four students here on May 12th that catapulted a few brave cries for change into a nation's clear and undeniable demand for reform. As evening approached at the end of a day of protests, marches and sit-ins by students calling for Suharto's resignation, police opened fire and killed Elang Mulya Lesmana, 19, and Hendriawan Sie, 20. An hour later, students still refusing to disband, were shot at from campus rooftops. More students were injured. Heri Hertanto, 23, and Hafidin Royan, 21, were killed.

Yudhie Haryono, a student activist in those days recalled to me, "My mother, like many parents at the time, forbid me from protesting or from getting involved in any way." Those parents had lived through the worst of Suharto's terror in 1965. These brave students had never known an Indonesia not under Suharto's rule. Nine days later, on May 21, 1998 Suharto resigned. He died on January 27, 2008. Due to declining health in the last decades of his life, he was deemed unfit to stand trial.

***

I am walking through the gently lit alleyways of *Nusa (type of flower) Indah* (beautiful – regarding scenery) in the Klender section of East Jakarta. I am with Desmon, the musician from Padang's *Pasar Seni* who can sing hundreds of rock songs. He is returning home for the first time in many years. At 32 years old, Desmon is a unique piece of work. He is almost sickly skinny, but he walks with a certain conviction, a confidence about himself that says nothing can touch him. He is a gifted guitarist and singer, and has always found creative ways to make a living for himself and his family from painting houses to making wedding invitations.

In Desmon's words, "The south is the wealthy area, the north side is the rough part with the most poverty, the west is an extension of the city center with corporate buildings and nightlife, and East Jakarta is the real Jakarta, the area filled with true neighborhoods." A neighborhood: the reason even the dirtiest, most crime ridden cities are worth keeping, a village inside a city where people take notice of each other and rely on one another.

On both sides of this alley, no wider than my outstretched arms, rivers of sewer dish water slither by. Huge rats are everywhere, rats that look like they are on steroids. A number of times I have to hold my foot mid-step to keep myself from stepping on one. Desmon watches me awkwardly making my way through his childhood lanes. "In some places you might bump into rats. Here the rats bump into you." Roaches and stray cats with crooked tails also crawl by showing their place in this labyrinth.

Nusa Indah is a large block of concrete. There are no backyards, front yards or grass. But that does not deter its residents from making the most of what they have. Every single porch is filled with potted plants, trees and flowers, injecting some bright color and a soothing tone, as if the residents of *Nusa Indah* felt an obligation to live up to their neighborhood's title. The greenery stretches upward and out across the lanes creating a botanical passageway that faintly shades you from the mid-day sun.

We come upon an old woman, her hair covered with a light brown *jilbab*, chatting with her neighbors. Desmon introduces me to his former Koran teacher. While the Koran is considered the most important book in the life of any Muslim, most Indonesian Muslims have never read it. The Koran has been published in different languages, including *Bahasa* Indonesian, but Muslim teachers claim that Arabic is the only true language for the Prophet Muhammad's message, and that any translation is nothing but a bastardized shadow of the truth. Desmon, out of no academic obligation or family pressure, spent enough afternoons on this old woman's porch to be able to read the words of Muhammad himself. She looks her old student up and down fondly and asks about his family. Another smiling woman illustrates how long she has known Desmon by pretending to swing a baby in her arms.

There are a few guys, who look like they just got off work as security guards, watching a soap opera on an outdoor television. They look at Desmon as if they are seeing a ghost. One slowly pronounces each syllable "Des-mon-Nus-an-tar-a." After a couple turns we come upon another old woman wearing a traditional batik dress and a black *jilbab*. Desmon bows slightly and respectfully puts her hand to his forehead. Here we are ordered to take a seat. This was Desmon's childhood stoop, the place where he and his friends hung out when there was nowhere else to go. This woman has daughters Desmon's age that I am sure she kept at a safe distance from him and his friends.

Bu Yetti looks at me, shaking her head and with a big grin points to Desmon, "He was bad." In the mid-'90s, when Desmon and his *Nusa Indah* crew were teenagers, heroine was introduced to their neighborhood. "We had no idea what it was. I'm not going to say we thought it was healthy for us, but we didn't know how bad it was either." Time would teach Desmon and his friends what heroine could do. By the time Jakarta reached its political boiling point in the spring of '98, *Nusah Indah* was already burning.

"My first hit of heroin cost 10,000 rupiah ($1). Within a few weeks you couldn't find it anywhere for less than 90,000 ($9)," Desmon recalls. Today a hit would cost much more, but the kids in the neighborhood are not saving their pennies. They are too haunted by the stories of Desmon's generation.

Desmon and his boys were hooked easily. When they could not afford the high prices drug dealers charged, they sold everything they owned to pay for it. Desmon sold his entire collection of '90s rock cassettes. Then they starting meeting in the afternoons with empty laundry bags to figure out what they could steal. "My neighbors would lock the doors when they saw me coming. No one could trust me."

In *Shantaram*, Gregory David Roberts, a former heroin addict, described the eyes of a junkie as "lightless as the eyes of Greek statues, as lightless as hammered lead, as lightless as a bullet hole in a dead man's back." Sadly, Desmon's wild eyes never shed that forewarning of tragedy, a misleading cover to the radiant soul behind them.

The adults in *Nusa Indah* did everything they could to combat the epidemic and its consequential horrors. They set up local checkpoints at the entrances to alleyways. There was always someone to make sure that no drug dealers or trespassers entered their alleyways at night. Neighbors took turns rotating as watchdog, regardless of whatever job they had to go to in the morning.

"One day I snuck into the local university and stole all of the air conditioner remote controls," Desmon confesses, "then I went and sold them on the street market for a couple bucks each, enough to get a hit that day."

Desmon, who lost his mother at age four and his father at eighteen, was one of the lucky ones in the neighborhood. After the death of his father, his stepmother sent him on a bus to Padang, Sumatra, which to him might as well have been Milwaukee. "A lot of people around here were happy to see me go." After some turbulent months with relatives, Desmon finally found his lot of redemption. Hidden behind a grocery store and across the street from the crashing waves of the Indian Ocean, he would go to the same spot every night to shiver and cry and beg Allah for one more chance, until finally he beat his heroin addiction and was able to live again.

The old woman looks at Desmon as if she is looking at her own son. She asks Desmon if he remembers different events. Desmon nods, and I try to catch as much of her Jakarta-laced Indonesian as I can. Then suddenly I understand every single word that comes out of the old woman's mouth. I understand them because they are all numbers, dates. She rambles them off, one after another, ". . . December 12, 1997, March 29, 1998, April 6, 1998, July 20, 1998, September 10, 1998, January 4, 1999. . ."

I look at Desmon for an explanation. "She is running through all the dates when kids from this neighborhood died."

Neither of them get emotional, and I am taken back by their composure. I try to picture this old woman, leaving her village as a scared, young girl to go make a better life for herself in the largest city of her country. And she did. She married, bought a small house in a neighborhood where people took pride in what they had and the future that was possible for their children.

And tonight she is sitting with one of the few surviving boys that used to run these alleyways, and remembering all the others who hung out in front of her house, passed flirting glances at her daughters and left this world all too early because one vicious drug managed to penetrate her Indonesian dream. Desmon estimates that more than two-thirds of the boys he grew up with died during the heroine years.

On the walk back to his stepmom's house Desmon points out houses where his friends lived. He has not visited any of their graves. "Someday I will. I am just not ready for it yet."

***

The next day morning Desmon's stepmother has a fresh plate of *rendang* waiting for us on the kitchen table underneath a hard plastic fly net. During my stay at a hotel on *Jalan* Jaksa I managed to catch bedbugs. I told Desmon to warn his family and tell them that I would be happy to find a hotel. His step-mom says that would be ridiculous and even Desmon's step-brother asks why I am making such a big deal out of telling everyone. I tell them that if I went home and there was even a chance of me having bedbugs my Mom would quarantine me at the far end of our backyard.

I grab some rice out of the hot electric rice cooker and help myself to a big breakfast before Desmon takes me on a short tour. We walk through the animal market where we see monkeys, rare birds and other animals in small cages. I try to take a picture of the animal cruelties around me, but the street vendors quickly stop me. "Buy the bird! Then you can take him home, put him in your bathtub and take as many pictures as you want." Another vendor butts in, "You want a picture, go to the zoo!"

Eventually we make our way to the Jakarta Train Station, the setting for some of Pramoedya's best short stories. I try to buy tickets for us to Yogyakarta (pronounced joke-jah-kar-ta), commonly referred to as "Jogja," for the next morning, but all the seats are taken and Desmon and I have no choice but to wait an extra day. As we walk back, Desmon gives me an overview of Indonesia's post-revolution presidents. In just six years three presidents came and went: BJ Habibe, the German-educated engineer who offered East Timor a referendum and consequently allowed for the first and only piece of Indonesia to break away. Then there was Gus Dur, the blind preacher, followed by Megawati Sukarnoputri, the daughter of Sukarno. Susilo Bambang Yudhoyono (SBY), a former general who earned a master's degree at Missouri University, took office in 2004, and would lead Indonesia for the following decade.[1] Desmon never tires of giving me a better understanding of his country.

That night we hang out outside of a t-shirt store owned by one of Desmon's friends in *Nusa Indah*. We all chip in a few rupiah and Eejum returns a few

---

[1] In 2014 Joko Widodo, known as Jokowi, took office. A true populist, Jokowi was evicted three times growing up and began paying his way through school at age 12 by working in his father's furniture store.

138

minutes later with three big plastic bags of *anggur* (red wine), priced at 33,000 rupiah ($3.30) a bag.

There are about ten guys, all grew up in the neighborhood, most of them in their mid or late-20s are a few years younger than Desmon. Those few years probably saved their lives. Desmon, Denny and Fadil grew up in the hard years. What separated Desmon, Denny and Fadil from the others is that they had family in other parts of the country. Denny was sent to live with an uncle in South Sumatra where hard drugs had not yet arrived. He beat his addiction. He lives at home with his parents now and plays the drums in a local band. He is an avid reader, and like many of this country's musicians, has an unquenchable thirst for knowledge. I quickly realize that I am not capable of answering his questions about Kant and Kierkegaard. He has trouble finding rewarding work. His friends say he needs more of an outlet for all of the philosophy he fills his head with.

Fadil's family sent him to a quiet village in Java. That decision was made after Fadil walked into the bathroom of a neighborhood mosque to do a hit. A group of men who were there to pray opened the door to the bathroom to find Fadil with his arm tied in a tunic and the needle in his hand. They gave him such a beating that his mother knew she had no choice, but to send him away.

Eejum was born with a face that screams juvenile delinquency, which must have contributed to his inability to be serious. When another friend from the neighborhood shows up, Eejum, who is much smaller than his friends, jumps up, slaps his hand and wishes him a happy birthday in English. I look over at Desmon. He says Eejum likes practicing the few English phrases he knows. I ask the guys if there any girls in *Nusa Indah* or if they already scared them all away. Eejum says there will be some girls coming later. Fadil and Denny start running through some of the beauties that roamed these alleyways in the '90s.

"Did you guys mess around with girls from the neighborhood when you were teenagers?"

"No".

"Seriously, why not?"

"Because it against the Koran."

I am having a hard time following. These are guys who robbed their neighbors and shot heroin in mosques, why would they decide to listen to that part of the Koran? They look at me as if the answer should be obvious.

"It is forbidden."

The Koran states that your afterlife will consist of roasting in a fiery pit of evil if you have pre-marital sex. Apparently the other commandments do not carry such severe punishments. I am not sure if they are being coy because they are shy in front of a group or if these former hood rats really were prudes.

They ask me about America, which they all think of as the "Land of Free Sex." I try to teach them that it is not like free Wi-Fi. American women are not sex-crazed animals waiting around in bars and clubs to be mounted.

The Javanese are known for their good manners and their tendency to avoid unpleasant or contentious topics. Sex seems to be a little too taboo for us to stay on the topic for long. One of the younger guys asks if I have ever been on a road trip in America. When I get hit with a question like that, asked with such innocence and wonder I can not help but feel a pang of longing in my heart. At moments like this, if I had $25,000, I would fly every one of them to New York, rent a van, buy them their fill of rice and drive west. Let them feel what it is like to be behind the wheel on a cornfield lined highway, stop in a bar in a rustic town, tell Desmon to take care of the jukebox, watch Denny share his philosophical arguments with cattle ranchers and little Eejum test his charm and "happy birthday" line on young girls wearing hoop earrings. See if American women live up to their expectations and learn what it is they miss most about home.

Instead, I settle for treating everyone to a couple more bags of wine. I take a ride with Kidoy to the store to pick them up. Although Kidoy is years younger than Desmon and did not know him well when he lived here, he says Desmon is a great friend and that he was so excited about his stay here that he is crashing at

141

Denny's parents' house for a few nights. Later, Desmon tells me Kidoy just wants to get away from his wife.

When we return, a couple cute local girls have shown up. They ask if I am single, and I tell them that as of very recently, I am. *"Bohong!* (Lie!)," one shouts. Indonesians are rarely shy about telling you they think you are lying. When I ask if they are single one responds, "I am single on Facebook."

We all hang out late into the night, sitting on the ground, benches and motorbikes, sharing stories and passing the *anggur* bags around. Fadil reminds me of my friends back home, sitting on a motorbike in the middle of everyone, constantly on the watch for someone or something to make fun of. When I look at Desmon, Denny and Fadil laughing together, I can not help but feel like they have already lived one life more than the rest of us.

As the morning sun sheds its light on *Nusa Indah,* the colors pulsating from each home's potted garden re-emerge, an emblem of *Nusa Indah* and a distinct beauty I would not find anywhere else. A beauty brimming with a nameless element that only someone whose eyes light up when they hear the phrase "the old neighborhood" could ever fully recognize.

Before we catch our train to Jogja, I buy two plants to give to Desmon's stepmom. Desmon grabs my backpack and leaves me clumsily holding both plants. "Sorry Kev, women buy plants. I can't be seen walking through *Nusa Indah* with a plant."

Old Batavia, Jakarta

Kantor Imigrasi

Jogja

My first trip to Jogja's (pronounced joke-jah) *Kantor Imigrasi* began civil enough. There was a machine at the entrance that gave me a number. I pressed 11 for Visa Renewal and the corresponding numbered ticket slid out, giving me my place in line. Then before I took a seat, a security guard directed me outside to buy the necessary forms, which cost 5,000 rupiah ($0.50). I was only sitting in the waiting room three minutes when my number was called. I was directed to *Locket* (Window) 11 where an older, studious-looking official was waiting for me. Maybe this renewal would turn out to be as easy as it should be.

I greet him and hand him my renewal papers and passport. After a few quick glances back and forth between my papers and me he looks up.

"Do you have a sponsor here in Yogyakarta?"

"No Pak, you see I was a professor at Andalas University in Sumatra. Currently I am writing a book, and I am being sponsored by the royal Prince of Ternate. I was told I could renew this visa anywhere in Indonesia."

He could not look less impressed. Jogja has its own sultan with a lineage that can be traced back over 250 years. When the Dutch finally left Indonesia in

1949, the Dutch Governor-General, too proud to shake hands with Sukarno, Hatta and rest of the new leadership, ceded his authority to the Sultan of Yogyakarta. The Sultan of Yogyakarta actually helped bankroll Indonesia it its early years after independence. Many of Jogja's residents still live in the area inside of the Sultanate's walls. The present Sultan was elected governor of the province of Yogyakarta in 1998 and has held the position ever since. In late 2010 when President SBY tried to abolish the power of the Sultanate in an attempt to institute a more uniform democratic system of government throughout the archipelago, the locals went wild. You can still find graffiti near the *Kraton* (Sultanate Palace) telling Jakarta to stay out of Jogja's affairs. Driving around the city it is easy to spot the Sultan's men, with their batik bandanas and *kris (traditional knife)* sticking out of their batik robes. The *Abdi Dalem* receive a salary of 5,000 rmb ($0.50) per month, but they take their job as seriously as a judge. They are considered the guardians of Javanese culture and tradition.

The official hands my papers back to me, with the Prince's autograph and all, and tells me that Yogyakarta is different from the rest of Indonesia. He tells me to come back when I have a local sponsor.

I have not made any friends in Jogja, but the kid who served me my *kopi susu* this morning seemed nice enough. I go back to *Toko Kopi* (Coffee Store) to see if he wants to be my sponsor.

It is always an awkward conversation that makes me feel like I am asking someone to marry me so I can get a green card. He agrees. I tell him I will pick him up on my rented motorbike at 10:00 tomorrow morning. I arrive at 9:45 and there is Asin waiting with his hair spiked, jeans that have been fashionably sliced up around the knees and a black heavy metal t-shirt. I tell him about my past problems with *kantor imigrasi* dress code and we swing by his house so he can change. When we get to the office we take our number and await our fate. *Locket* 11 again. Asin and I walk up. The same immigration official sternly reads through my sponsorship application. He walks away and a fat, jolly official returns with my papers in his hand.

"Selamat pagi."

"Selamat pagi Bung."

"I see you want to stay in Jogja a little longer."

"Yes, this is a great town."

"Oh yes, thank you. But first I just need you to come into the backroom and we are going to have a little interrogation."

I start wondering if maybe the word interrogation does not have such harsh implications in Indonesian. *Bung*, still with a big smile on his chubby face, makes it sound like we are going to have a picnic together. I tell Asin that I will be back in a little while and whisper in his ear, "Don't say nothing to nobody."

Chubby *Bung* is behind his desk typing every word of our interrogation into his computer. First question: "What is your relation to the gentleman, Asin, outside?"

"Asin and I met a few days ago at a quaint little café called *Toko Kopi*. He served me my coffee. We started talking, realized we have similar tastes in music and have become very close friends."

"What is the relation between Asin and the Prince of Ternate?"

"As far as I know, there is none. But maybe I will introduce them some day."

"Is this the Prine's signature on this form?"

"Yes it is." To this day, I firmly believe that no matter how many times you scan and copy someone's signature it is still their signature.

"Why do you want to stay in Indonesia so long?"

"I am writing a book about my trip across the country. I am travelling from Aceh to Papua."

"Aceh to Papua," Chubby Bung repeats.

I probably could have left out the names of those two places. Government officials are always wary of foreigners stirring up trouble in areas known for their regional rebellions. After a few follow up questions we move on to more crucial aspects of the interrogation.

"Why is your last name Lee?"

"It's a rare Irish name. My grandparents were from Ireland."

"Have you ever been to China?"

"Umm, yeah sort of," looking at my passport in Chubby *Bung's* hand, "I lived there for two years."

After each question Chubby *Bung* slowly types my answer, followed by a translation in Indonesian. Eventually I try to answer each question in both languages to make it easier on him. He then types his next question in English, along with an Indonesian translation. About 4-7 minutes pass in between each question of the interrogation.

Finally after a long typing pause, *Bung* prints out the results of our interrogation and has me sign at the bottom. He shakes my hand and tells me that they will review my application and that I should return in a couple days. That does not sound so bad.

As I walk out of the office I wonder if they took little Asin to be interrogated too. I hope it is not like the movies where he gets the mean, sadistic interrogator and comes out all bloodied and screaming like a madman, and then he sees me squeaky clean and assumes I am a rat.

Asin is where I left him listening to heavy metal on his MP3 player.

Over the next ten days I make five trips to Jogja's *Kantor Imigrasi* and three to a downtown immigration law office, often transporting sealed envelopes, which I am told contain important documents regarding my visa, between the two offices. I wonder if what I am carrying even has anything to do with my visa or if they just think it is amusing to have a *bule* mail courier. I have been wearing my only pair of pants for over a week now because I never have enough time to leave them at a laundry hut.

Each trip the officials at *Kantor Imigrasi* say they will text me the next day to tell me when I should return to pick up my passport. Since I have never had a phone in Indonesia I give them Asin's number. Every day I go by *Toko Kopi,* and Asin tells me he has not received a text yet. Then I ride twenty-five minutes out to *Kantor Imigrasi,* where no one looks excited to see me.

On a Thursday afternoon I make my last trip to Jogja's *Kantor Imigrasi.* An official has informed me that today is my judgment day. I will leave the office today with my passport in hand. Whether or not it will have a new visa renewal inside of it, giving me another thirty days, is still unknown. If it does not, then I must quickly exit the country and pay a $50 fine for each day I have overstayed my last visa.

While I walk in, I realize I have lost the altar boy mentality, and I give off more of an air that says if I don't get this visa I am going to go ape-shit crazy. My number is called. I tell the official why I am here, as if he does not recognize me. He tells me to have a seat and that someone will be with me in a moment.

As I watch the official walk to a back room I am instantly reminded of a short period of my childhood. I was six years old and my parents had just bought our first VCR. Forget about having to fight with my brother to switch the channel to the Care Bears, now I could just pop in a VHS tape any time I wanted.

When my neighbor, Violet, would come over to play I could not let her see how easy this magical machine worked. So while she sat on our rug waiting I would put on a big show. First I would make it look like I was quickly pressing every button on the remote control. I was not actually pressing any buttons because I did not know what they did and did not want to screw anything up. I told Violet this was a code that only worked for my VCR.

Then I would carefully place the VHS tape inside the VCR and quickly pull my hand back before the strange machine's teeth snapped my little fingers off. I would hit the power button, but not the play button causing a blue screen to appear. I would proceed to grunt and nod my head knowingly as if the problem was very complex, but of course one that I could fix. Then I would eject the tape, hand it to Violet and tell her to gently blow into the space where the thin string of film connected to the two white wheels. I would launch into a furious spectacle of code punching, both on the remote and the actual VCR, extremely careful not to actually press any buttons. Then I would tell Violet that I think I figured it out and to hand me the tape immediately. My first method of impressing a female only worked for a week until Violet's family also bought a VCR.

"Mr. Lee!"

I am shaken out of my reverie. The chubby official that interrogated me is calling me over to *Locket* 9. I walk over to learn my fate.

"Mr. Lee, we have reviewed your application, investigated the background of your sponsors and your relationship to them and examined the record of our recent interrogation. Here is your passport. Enclosed is a visa renewal allowing you to remain in Indonesia for thirty more days."

I take my passport with a look on my face more stunned than little Violet's when that VHS tape starting rolling and Funshine Bear came sliding down the rainbow.

6
Jogja

When I am not busy making trips to *kantor imigrasi*, I go around the city's sights with Desmon. At 4:45 one morning, we drive out under a huge full moon to see the sunrise at Borobudur, a Buddhist temple built over an estimated 75-year period at some time between the seventh and ninth centuries and abandoned for hundreds of years under volcanic ash by a local population that had converted to Islam. It is a pyramid structure with four sides, each as long as a football field, reaching 115 feet high with over 500 Buddha statues. As we walk around each level of the volcanic stone structure, we are ascending a symbol of the different levels of enlightenment. While I am often uninterested in must-see sights, Borobudur is easily one of the most impressive man-made structures I have ever experienced.

We stay at a Minang artist's house that Desmon knows from Padang. Romi is about our age and has established himself as a painter in Jogja. He lives in a spacious studio surrounded by rice fields, just a ten minute drive outside of the city center. There is one mattress in each of the two bedrooms, a small kitchen and a wide hallway filled with his large canvas paintings. As I walk around Romi's place I can not think of a more perfect setting for an artist; to be surrounded by your own work everywhere you look, a mattress to sleep on, a kitchen for when you feel like cooking, a *warung* up the road with delicious 6,000 rupiah ($0.60) meals, a motorbike to take you to see culture in the city or nature in the other direction.

Then Romi shows me a picture of his wife and baby daughter, who are visiting his in-laws in West Sumatra. I search his place in vain for a crib, diapers, toys, oversized stuffed animals. It baffles me that Romi can have a family and still manage to keep such simplicity in his life.

One day, while Romi stays home to paint, we rent bicycles with a Belgian teacher, Bert, that has been living in Jogja for a couple years. I douse every exposed part of my body in sunblock and we ride out through the surrounding green rice fields. Desmon can not remember the last time he rode a bicycle, but seems to get the hang of it easily. At one point he falls behind, but later passes us by holding on to the back of a truck.

After a couple hours we stop at a bamboo hut to cool off. We ask Bert what is was like during the eruptions of Mount Merapi in 2010, which resulted in

353 deaths and forced 350,000 people in nearby villages to relocate. Bert says that there was little worry of Mount Merapi, located 17 miles north of Jogja, having any devastating effect on the actual city. Bert knew this because he was following the news from BBC and other foreign media outlets. The Javanese, who hold on to many pre-Islam animist beliefs, were watching local anchors interview sorcerers and witch doctors who were predicting Armageddon and terrifying an already tense population.

Bert asks me what my plans are when I get to Papua. We discuss the human rights abuses, the atmosphere of intimidation and corruption that forced Papua's inclusion into Indonesia in 1969 and the Free Papua Movement. Desmon looks up and says, "Foreigners are always trying to stir up trouble in Indonesia," and then goes back to sipping his drink.

I am a little surprised by Desmon's comment. He has as much knowledge of Indonesian history as most professors, and I have never known him to be sensitive to criticism against his government. But I begin to see that despite all of Desmon's critiques of his young country, he still holds a fierce pride in being Indonesian. It is insulting to him to hear two foreigners discuss Papua as if it should not be a part of Indonesia, especially when neither of us has been there. Months later when I told Desmon of my conversations with Papuans and how none of them really wanted to be a part of Indonesia, he was much more open to the discussion.

But for that afternoon, Desmon only saw two foreigners convinced that the news from their part of the world was right. He came from a country that was ruled and pillaged during his grandparent's generation and for many generations before that. He is proud that almost this whole archipelago, with more than twice as many islands as the entire Caribbean, was all part of his country, in the same way I was proud of California, even if we stole it from Mexico, or the Grand Canyon, even if everything around it was once the home of proud Native-American tribes that my culture decimated.

We ride back into town. Old *becak* drivers fill the narrow streets. Most of the tin carts are filled with mothers and children as these aged, but healthy men work their legs, pedalling their customers around. Jogja's *becak* drivers are the gentlest people I have ever seen working in a mass transit industry. When they ask you if you need a ride they almost whisper to you, as if they do not want to wake a nearby sleeping baby. Desmon teaches me to respond *"Ora, Mas."* (Javanese: No, Sir) It always makes them smile to hear a *bule* speak Javanese.

After passing the ninth century Prambanan Hindu Temple, we turn on to a main street and a woman on a bicycle yells toward me, *"Temanmu jatuh!"* (Your friend fell) I look back and do not see Desmon anywhere. Bert and I turn our bikes round. Desmon is sitting on a wooden bench on the side of the road holding a bag of ice against his arm. His face is filled with rage. He points to a young man with a nervous

156

smile and tells me that this guy ran him off the road with his motorbike. As Desmon explains what happened, I can sense that it is irritating him that I might be assuming this happened because he does not know how to ride a bike.

I recall a line from the Lonely Planet travel guide, "Accidents usually result in large pay-offs or pricey lawsuits and a number of drivers are killed every year by angry crowds exacting mob justice following an accident." Desmon looks like he would not mind taking part in some mob justice. The driver approaches us and starts asking us a laundry list of questions:

"*Dari mana?*" (Where are you from?)

"*Apa lakukan di Jogja?*" (What are you doing in Jogja?)

"*Suka Jogja?*" (Do you like Jogja?)

I know why he is doing this. It makes it harder for you to be furious with someone after you have just answered all of their questions that were asked with a big smiling face. Desmon is too polite to ignore him, but he answers his questions in short responses still glaring out at the road. A couple times the young man tries to hand Desmon a wad of small bills. Desmon swats the money away.

I think that this is part of the custom, that Desmon should refuse the first few offers until the defendant realizes that Desmon means business and offers a more suitable settlement. I feel like asking for a play-by-play explanation of how it works, but I do not want to irritate Desmon more. Eventually Desmon accepts a few bills, which looks to about 60,000 rupiah ($6). Still nervously smiling, the young guy leaves with his girlfriend after repeatedly saying how nice it was to meet us, and that he hopes we enjoy our time in Jogja.

I ask Desmon if he wants to go see a doctor. He looks over at me, "I need to see a shaman."

I did not realize that Desmon believed in traditional medicine. I ask a woman if she knows of any shamans or traditional healers in the area. She points to the shack behind us and says that he should be back very soon. We wait in the same spot. A man with no eyes and scars all over his body stumbles past us with a walking stick. I suggest to Desmon that we let him go first. Desmon looks at me like I am an idiot.

"That's the shaman, Kev."

After about twenty minutes Desmon walks out, claiming to feel a little better. I do not bring up Papua or our bike ride for the rest of the trip.

***

One night Desmon and I get dinner at one of the small outdoor *warungs* on *Jalan* Malioboro. One of the most famous streets in all of Indonesia and a trademark of Jogja, *Jalan* Malioboro is overrun with tourists shopping in its batik, jewelry and souvenir stores during the day, but the area reclaims its charm at night.

We sit on matted floors and eat *pecel lele* (catfish with vegetables) off a table slightly raised off the floor. Talented street musicians roam the area. One young musician with jeans and a ripped t-shirt starts playing his guitar and singing an Indonesian song in front of our table. I tell Desmon that I think I listened to this guy play on my first trip to Jogja over three years ago. Desmon gives me a patronizing nod.

I tell the musician that I think I remember him. He nods, but I can tell he does not believe me either. I ask him if he knows any Beatles or Elvis songs. He starts playing "Let It Be," followed by "You were Always on my Mind."

When I first started travelling Asia, someone advised me to carry small cultural tokens from America to give as gifts. My mother owns more Elvis paraphernalia than a retro 1950s diner. While most of it would be too much of a hassle to travel with (I was not going to walk through customs with life-sized cut outs), she did have a few collections of Elvis playing cards she was willing to part with. After checking on Amazon to find that each card was worth about $1 and would not fund her grandkids' education, I decided to travel with them and give them to any musicians I appreciated. I would always try my best to say in their language that this is the greatest musician ever born in my country.

I have gifted musicians from Rangoon to Hohhot with my mother's entire 1977 collection and many more from her 1990s collections. I take one of the few remaining Elvis cards out of my pocket and hand it to Koko. Before I can give my one-liner he shouts, *"Aku ingat kamu!"* (I remember you!)

He starts feverishly searching through his wallet and eventually pulls out an Elvis card from the 1977 collection. Desmon is laughing his head off. The card has obviously been left in his jeans at least one laundry day. The colors on both sides have been bleached, but you can still make out that iconic smile.

Later that night, we go hang out at the *Asmara* (Love) Restaurant. An old friend of Desmon's is performing in a '50s rock band that he formed with a group of teenagers. The youngest member of the band is just 14. He sits on his drum banging away and making severe eye contact with the crowd. A European woman comments to me how irresistible he is going to be in a few years. His brother, who is just a couple years older, plays the guitar and sings. One of their friends plays the bass and sings backup. Riezky, who could care less that he is twice the age of the other members, sings and routinely takes a couple songs off to move around the crowd.

The whole band dons tight blue jeans, plaid shirts, sideburns and gelled hair. They sing songs by Elvis, Hank Williams and Roy Orbison and others. I sit down with the parents of the two brothers in the band. The father tells me that he was a failed musician because all he could play was Led Zeppelin and the music of that era. He wanted his boys to have a specialty, a genre that no one else could play. I imagine in the middle of Indonesia, his boys are an anomaly. I question if the boys are as enthusiastic as their father about this choice or if they are secretly dying to shave those sideburns. When the band takes a break, they join us at our table. The boys are filled with questions about America and rock music and especially about my trip to Graceland. I can not keep up with their questions about '50s rock artists, and I am shocked that teenagers in Indonesia could know so much more than me about the music of my parents' generation.

Suddenly Desmon and Riezky approach the table wide-eyed, talking a mile a minute about a guy named Butet that is at the back of the restaurant right now. They say something about him being a cultural critic and a comedian and how he imitates Suharto. Then they grab me and bring me over to his table. *Mas* Butet Kartaredjasa is a little guy with big psychedelic framed glasses.

Desmon introduces me as a writer who is currently writing a book about Indonesia. I can see I am the excuse that Desmon and Riezky needed to approach this table. *Mas* Butet asks us to sit down. Desmon and Riezky pick up where they left off in reciting Butet's biography. They go on about him being a cultural critic and imitating Suharto and how funny this man in front of me is. They seem to expect me to be able to have everything I need to interview this apparently famous man. *Mas* Butet just stares at me through his glasses with a serious look. I am at a loss for words. I consider saying, "So, tell me a joke," but decide better. *Mas* Butet, sensing my unease, shakes my hand and says, "Google me and then come to my house tomorrow."

That night I heed Butet´s advice. I learn that not only does almost every Indonesian know *Mas* Butet, but most remember where they were when they watched Butet on national television imitating and poking fun of the man who ruled their country with an iron fist for over three decades – while that man was still in power. Years later, he started a comedy show that ran Saturday Night Live style skits, often poking fun at the political dynamics of his country. Mas Butet Kartaredjasa appears to be the Jon Stewart and Stephen Colbert of his country. He also writes critiques on the talent pool in Indonesia from music, art, acting and stand-up comedy.

Desmon, Romi and I arrive at *Mas* Butet´s house around midday. Romi can not believe that I have only been in Jogja a few days and already have an invitation to Butet Kartaredjasa's house. *Mas* Butet introduces us to his wife and daughter, leads us to courtyard in the middle of his home and offers us coffee.

"Your name is not a typical Indonesian male name. How did your parents choose this name?"

"My father was in Vietnam when he heard a song called *Butet.* The song touched him deeply. He immediately sent a telegram to my mother telling her that his son's name must be Butet."

"Who were the people who influenced your worldview most?"

"My mother and father."

"You chose a different path from what your father wanted for you (Butet's father wanted him to follow in his footsteps as a painter). When you look at Indonesian society, do you believe more young Indonesians need to step out of the expectations of family and society?"

"My parents were not typical parents." (I sense that Butet has his reasons for being coy).

"What gave you the courage to go on television and poke fun of a dictator that had ruled your country for over 30 years?"

"I had been imitating Suharto since the early 80s. 1998 was just first time I did it on stage."

"Right, but what gave you the courage to go on stage and imitate him?"

"I talked to many people high up. They told me I would be okay, and I talked to people who had an escape route ready for me if I wasn't."

"To Singapore?" Romi quips, making everyone laugh. Romi is making a reference to Muhammad

Nazaruddin, the treasurer of Indonesia's Democratic Party, who was on the run at the time. After being charged with corruption, he fled to Singapore and leaked information to the media that clearly implicated many high ranking members of Indonesia's government and military on corruption charges. Nazaruddin would spend months making a mockery out of Indonesia's government, particularly the president's party, before being tracked down and arrested in Colombia.

"Besides the obvious reasons for comedy, did the comic strip *sentilan-sentilun* (no translation) have something else it was trying to achieve?"

"Absolutely, I wanted to make critics out of Indonesians."

Reflecting on that interview, I later realized how important Butet's work was. I remember all those brilliant young college girls I had spoken with about the Koran. I would egg them on to debate me on stories like the husband who for no apparent reason told his wife she was forbidden from attending her beloved mother's funeral. The woman obeys her husband. The moral of the story: obey your husband. Why could I not get one of those girls to admit that part of the Koran does not make any sense? The most rebellious answer I could pry out was, "Well the man I am going to marry would not do that." Questioning them about the fact that that man would also have a right to marry three more women did not illicit any more of a criticism on the Koran.

"Many people around the world look at Indonesia as a battleground for conservative Islamic beliefs versus more liberal Western views. How do you see this battle playing out?"

"I am Christian. My wife is Muslim. (In most parts of Indonesia one of them would have had to convert, at least on paper.) I do not want to take a side on this issue. I just want to make Indonesians question things. I want to make them become critics."

"I read that you gave President Yudhoyono a book you had written called *Presiden Guyonan* (Joke President). Can you explain the motivation behind this?"

"All I know is he didn't read it."

"If you had to plan a trip for a friend visiting Indonesia, what would be the first place you would suggest going to gain an understanding of your country?"

"The market."

"Why?"

"Because all aspects of Indonesian society are present in a traditional market."

Before we leave, I give Mas Butet a couple pearl bracelets for his wife and daughter and thank him for his hospitality. He gives me a signed copy *Presiden Guyonan* (Joke President). As we get up, *Mas* Butet looks over to Desmon and Romi, "He Googled me, didn't he?"

***

That night while Desmon is nursing his bike wounds, I wander over to a reggae bar downtown off *Jalan* Malioboro. Across the street there are at least fifty young Indonesians sitting outside a convenience store and listening to the reggae that finds its way out of the club. Inside there is a mix of Indonesians and Westerners and a live local band playing some of its own songs and a lot of Bob Marley. I stand at the end of the bar, and try to get enough *Anker* beer in me so I do not look like the stiffest guy in the club. Most of the clientele are males and our eyes all ricochet off the small handful of cute college girls. In many parts of Indonesia, women see no difference between going to a bar and being a prostitute. Fortunately Jogja is a bit more liberal.

After my fourth *Anker,* my head starts bobbing slightly and my knees prove that they do actually bend. I start singing Bob Marley's words to myself in my lowest voice. And then the cutest girl in the bar walks up behind me and says, "Sing louder."

I hang out with Kumala a few nights during my last week in Jogja. She is an anthropology student at Gajah Madah University, one of the top five schools in the country. She has wavy black hair, bronzed skin, a button nose, and the cutest smile you could ever find. She also has the sweetest, babyish voice. *"Me da-DDY!"* The *da* in a low tone and the *DDY* jumps up like an excited child who was just been given ice cream. "If my da-DDY finds out I hang out late at clubs he will stop sending me money for school." She says Bali the same way, "When I was living in ba-LI!"

On my last night in town she is wearing a low cut t-shirt that reveals her cleavage. Kumala has a free spirit. She is confident and laughs easily. She has no problem holding my hand when we walk down *Jalan* Malioboro. But Kumala is terrified of her parents finding out how she is living here. Dancing at clubs, sometimes finishing a whole beer in one night, meeting boys and holding hands with them, living *la vida loca*.

Kumala is from a more conservative part of the country. Her family moved to Bali when she was in high school and she likes to call herself Balinese. Kumala does not fit the mold of any Indonesian ethnic group. I know I have never met anyone in Indonesia that talks like her. Another reason she says she is Balinese is because of the strange way Indonesians are able to trace you to someone they know, which could mean someone telling her father about her scandalous lifestyle. I have seen, more than once, two Indonesians ask a series of questions that leads to them knowing the same person in a tiny village 1,000 miles away, but still I feel like she is being a little paranoid.

That night we both invite a few of our friends out to dinner. Kumala plays the Balinese part until one of her friends slips up and reveals that Kumala is originally from Sumatra. Before she knows it, one of guys at the table is calling his wife to confirm that she and Kumala were a year apart from each other at the same grade school and is calculating how far the parents of the two girls live from each other. Kumala covers her face with her hands.

When Kumala is in Bali, her parents give her a curfew of 11:00 p.m. and allow her to bathe in a swimsuit at the beach. In Sumatra she must be home before sundown and cover her long black hair with a *jilbab,* revealing nothing but her hands and face. While a strong social structure allows Indonesians to lean on one another in times of need, it can also play a major role in regulating their lives.

After dinner, everyone wants to go to a karaoke bar, but I convince Kumala to take a ride around town with me. She grabs her helmet and jumps on the back of my motorbike. We cruise around the Sultan's grounds and stop at a lively park called *Alun Alun Kidul.*

There is a ritual at *Alun Alun Kidul* that Kumala wants me to try. I have to keep my eyes closed while Kumala spins me around a few times and then find my way through a forty-foot space between two big trees, which are the centerpiece and pride of this park. You must make a wish before attempting the feat, and if you can make it through the trees within three tries, your wish will come true. Kumala reminds me to trust my instincts and assures me if I am in any danger she will protect me. As I make my wish, I stare for a second at what is still concealed by her low cut shirt.

On my first two attempts, I walk straight out of the park. On my third and final attempt, Kumala basically drags me through the two trees and then congratulates me on a job well done. I ask her if she wants to try. She gives me a look that says, "Do I look like a dumb tourist to you?"

After a couple laps around the park of listening to the live music from different corners, we sit down on a bamboo mat. We order a couple *kopi susus*. I have a few *Bintangs* in me, and we have already kissed a few times on our walk around the park. I figure this may be as close as I will feel to a girl this trip so we let the conversation slip into areas that would normally be off limits between a *bule* and a Muslim Indonesian girl.

There is one nagging question that young women in Indonesia have about these men from the Western world that pass through their country. Kumala asks, "Are you Americans really the dogs the movies make you out to be?"

"Absolutely we are. The movies don't tell the half of it." No one likes having their stereotypes disproved, and there is no way she would believe me if I tried.

I teach her about the 4 bases in America and tell her that if she pays attention it is only awkward this one time, and then she can talk about this with *bules* more easily in the future. I want to ask her about female circumcision. I have no idea what the word is in Indonesian so I end up making a snipping motion with my fingers near the zipper of her jeans. She understands. She says she remembers her baby sister crying one day. Her mother explained what had happened to Kumala's sister and told her that the same procedure had been done to her.

"I don't remember it because I was only a few months old."

"How do you feel about that being done to you?"

"I think it's better they did it then. If they did it when I was older I would have big pain."

"Do you believe it is wrong?"

"It is custom. It is not for me to say if it is right or wrong."

"Why do you think this is done?"

"My mom says because it helps us to control our passion. This way we do not get very hot and lose control of ourselves. But I also heard that it can take away some of the enjoyment."

Female Genital Circumcision/Mutilation (FGM) is not part of Islamic Law. It is an ancient, ritual that actually predates Islam. Abigail Haworth, a journalist for The Guardian, witnessed a mass mutilation ceremony at a Javanese school in 2006. She watched as an untrained *dukun* (witch doctor/ shaman) cut off the tip of the clitoris of 248 girls aged from five months to twelve years old. Each young girl on the assembly line was held down by women, who like Kumala, believed that the procedure was necessary to control a woman's sexual urges. At this ceremony, the procedure was performed with what Haworth described as nail scissors. In more remote parts of the country a piece of sharpened bamboo is used.

Indonesia's parliament claims that banning the procedure will just push it underground and force FGM to be performed in less sanitary environments. Hospitals have begun offering the procedure as a package deal that includes necessary infant vaccinations, and many religious leaders encourage the practice.

In 2012 the U.N. banned Female Genital Mutilation and classified it as any practice that alters or removes any part of the genitals. Leading media outlets, such as the Jakarta Globe have pressured the government to abide by this international law. Regardless of what the law states, it will be a long time before the misconceptions held by so many Indonesians are disproved.

"In America and many parts of the world it is called Female Genital Mutilation and is considered a violation of human rights."

Kumala's mouth tightens, and I can tell I have offended her. No one likes to hear their country, never mind their own mother being accused of human rights abuses.

"Well that is your country. This is Indonesia."

I try not to let the night be ruined by such a contentious topic. I remember once being given a fascinating tour of a staunch Muslim town by a college student wearing a *jilbab*. She was eager to show me around her neighborhood and had many questions about America. Toward the end of a great day, we saw a young boy running around wearing an Osama bin Laden t-shirt. I knew that there were parts of Indonesia that viewed bin Laden as a type of Robin Hood figure and knew as much about his politics as anyone wearing a Che Guevara shirt might know about his. But I still could not help but be appalled by it.

When I asked her about the shirt, she was vague. When I expressed my own opinions about the man who masterminded the deaths of 3,000 innocent Americans and told her what that infamous day was like in America, she brushed me off saying, "That is America's problem." (I should note that the majority of Indonesians view bin Laden as a terrorist, and that in general, Indonesians have an unmatched disdain for terrorists because of the terrible name that they give to Muslims.)

Kumala and I leave the issue there and finish our *kopi susus*. We walk back to the other side of the park and sit down in front of a group of teenagers singing and playing their guitars atop their motorbikes. Kumala looks over at me, "You know you are the first guy I have ever kissed in a park." I smile, and in standard fashion for me, can not think of anything to say.

She laughs, "You will just find a more beautiful girl somewhere else in Indonesia."

"I hope so."

She laughs harder, "I like that answer."

Our flirting goes no farther than *Alun Alun Kidul* Park. Mainly because Kumala has certain morals and partly because if she did consent, I have no idea where I would take her anyway. Even in Jogja, showing up at certain hotels at 3:00 AM with a local woman who is not your wife is not a good idea.

She gets on the back of my motorbike, and we circle a few of the Sultan's streets. She reminds me that I can not hug or kiss her anywhere near her house. I nonchalantly mention that there may be a quiet place we could go in the southern part of town, but she just continues giving me directions to her house. Our four-day relationship ends as innocently as it began.

We say goodbye, and I drive back to Romi's place with the ring of "da-DDY!" and "ba-LI!" in my ears. By the time I get home, my mood has soured, and all I can think about is the stupid walk through the two trees and how it does not make your wish come true.

Jogja

Jalan Malioboro, Jogja

7

Surabaya, East Java

Desmon flies home from Jogja and lackdaddy I'm back on the road *sendiri* (alone). I send out a couch surfing request and end up in a spacey, loft with a bunch of young Indonesian guys and girls. So many people come in and out of the apartment, it is impossible to tell who actually lives here. My first day, Karina, who does not live at the loft, offers to take me around the city. It is always exciting to explore a city that everyone says has absolutely nothing to see. I do not bother to make note of the polluted humid air, the traffic, the drab buildings or any other negative aspect. I am just eager to find one corner with a speck of beauty to marvel at so I can laugh at how all the other tourists can be so blind.

Surabaya is Indonesia's second largest city and is known as the City of Heroes for the strategic role it played in the Indonesian Revolution. The town is strewn with statues and parks dedicated to these revolutionary leaders. I was shocked to see how many Indonesians around the country could easily rattle off the names of more than twenty revolutionary leaders. There is Martha Christina in Ambon, who took up arms against the Dutch and while being transported aboard a slave ship refused to accept food or medicine. She died just two days before her eighteenth birthday. There is Pattimura, with his stone face holding a long, flat sword across his body in the picture on Indonesia's most common bill, the 1,000 rupiah ($0.10). Actually, now that I think of it, most Indonesian bills feature guys that look they are ready to give someone a beating.

If there is one bond that that unites all of these islands, all of these people, it is that they were conquered by the Dutch. A common enemy, even if that enemy disappeared more than sixty years ago, is always a solid way to promote unity. And what better way than calling the regional heroes, heroes to all of Indonesia? Even the name of Karina's university, *Universitas Sebalas November* (November 11th University) is a tribute to an important day of battle in Indonesia's revolution.

We stop in at the House of Sampoerna, a cigarette factory and cigarette museum in one. At one point I am watching the assembly line of women pack cigarette cloves with tobacco, seal them tightly and fill Sampoerna packs with them. I have never seen human hands move at anything close to this speed.

That night most of the loft and a few others go to an Irish pub with live music and good draft beers on tap. There are men and women hanging out at the bar on stools and not just at the surrounding tables. The band is playing rock songs in English and Indonesian. After a few conversations I see that Surabaya has some of the most laid-back, open-minded people in the country. Dating is dating, not just a search for the most suitable mate. Drinking at bars appears to be acceptable for males and females, and the city is not shy about staying up all hours of the night.

I get most of the loft eating peanut butter and apple or peanut butter and *pisang goreng* (fried banana) sandwiches. I take orders in the morning and make sandwiches for everyone. Then I watch a couple episodes of *Modern Family* with Winda, who is from Kalimantan. I start feeling guilty about wasting so much time each day until a Canadian couch surfer comes by and manages to watch four movies per day.

Eventually I find my little corner of Surabaya with a speck of beauty. Just a few blocks from the loft, *Taman Bukul* (Bukul Park) is about the size of a football field, filled with children's rides, green soccer patches, *warungs* and juice stands. Lining the outside of the park is a wide path where street vendors sit on the adjacent grass selling their goods. I introduce myself to a few of them and tell them that I am also a street vendor. They make room for me, clearing about six feet along the walkway, and for the next three weeks I have my place to sell.

There are a lot of vendors selling t-shirts, wallets, jewelry and *martabak* (minced mutton, egg and onion fried and stuffed inside a paper thin bread).   To my left is an old woman who sells cups of *kopi* and little snacks. Everything she sells can be bought with one picture of Pattimura's stone face and sword. The guy to my right is about my age and sells tribal bracelets and watches. Even though Sundays are the busiest selling day he always takes off to be with his daughter. I arrive in the evenings, usually after eating a dish of delicious *gado-gado* (an array of fresh boiled vegetables covered in a spicy brown peanut sauce) at one of the nearby *warungs*. Everyone else has been selling for many hours. They all smile when they see me.

The couples and families wandering around *Taman Bukul* usually do a double take when they see me sitting on the ground in front of my pearls. Sometimes the children notice me first and tug at their mother's dress pointing and whispering, *"Bu, bule bule!"* Most of them want to hear my story. American, not married, 29, I don't know why I'm not married, traveling Indonesia from Aceh *ke* Papua, hoping to write a book about it.

Sometimes they look at the pearls too, and I get to work my magic. *"Kalung, anting-anting, galung, mutiara asling, cantik pada kamu!"* (Necklace, earrings, bracelet, real pearls, beautiful on you!) A lot of people buy, a much higher percentage than the customers that stop by my table in New York. Almost no one buys anything without bargaining. Some just pick out a necklace and earrings, ask for a discount and take whatever price I give them. Others hang around for hours testing my patience by matching dozens of pieces and asking what the best price is I can do for each. Every once in awhile I slip up and give a better discount than I mean to. They immediately recognize it and jump to ask me why I can not do the same deal with the other two pieces. One young guy openly encourages his girlfriend to flirt with me to get him a better deal.

I hated the bargaining when I first arrived in Asia and still do not enjoy it when I am on the buyer's side of the table, but the seller's side is more fun. I can work with their proposed price. I can refuse that price, but offer to throw a bracelet in as *hadiah* (gift) or I can tell them to take a hike and find someone else at *Taman Bukul* that sells pearls at these prices.

While *Taman Bukul* might not be the most traditional of markets, I can still see what *Mas* Butet meant when he said that all aspects of Indonesian society are present here. You have every class of people. You can see the yearning for more that has been intensified with Western influence. You also can see the contentment with life that must come from generations of growing your own *nasi*, not staying in the sun too long and just being happy with what you have. You have every ethnicity. In my two weeks at *Taman Bukul* I meet people from all eight of Indonesia's major regions except for Papua. As a professor friend once quipped, "If you want to see Papuans, you go to Papua."

I am touched at how the other vendors are so happy to see me make a sale, often encouraging my customers to buy. On three separate nights at *Taman Bukul* I sold over 500,000 rupiah ($50) worth of pearls in just a few hours. I am sure most of these vendors did not make that much money all week. Yet they seemed more enthusiastic about selling my goods than they did their own.

I do my best to express my appreciation, buying coffees for some of my best customers and anytime a vendor expresses interest in my pearls, encouraging them to barter with their own merchandise. One night I trade a single pearl on a chain for two Surabaya t-shirts, one with a *becak* and another with the two animals that Surabaya owes its name to, a *sura* (Javanese: snakc) and a *baya* (Javanese: crocodile). By my second night there, I feel at ease walking to the public bathroom, leaving my treasure in their hands and knowing that my trust means more to them than anything else I could give them.

Some nights, someone from the loft will stop by and keep me company. I always try to give them some money or merchandise for sitting with me and helping when I do not completely understand one of my customers. They vehemently refuse any money, but before I leave Surabaya I get each of them to accept a parting gift. One night Karina gives me one of the nicest compliments I have ever received, "You know before you came, I think all of us at the loft thought that working like this was kind of a peasant's job, or at least a little below us. Now everyone thinks that selling in *Taman Bukul* is cool."

Each time I laid down my mat of jewelry, my goal was to make enough money to fund at least one day's expenses and to have one good conversation. I did not know it at the time, but I would end up making all of the money I needed (half of the trip's total expenses) by selling the pearls and stones, mostly on the closing leg of my trip in Jogja, Surabaya, Ambon and Papua. I would go almost the last two months of the trip without needing an ATM.

When John Steinbeck was in Mexico he loved to *vacilar*, a Spanish word, which he may have falsely translated to mean that you are going somewhere, but the place you are going does not even need to exist. I often wondered if my destination existed.

My nights at *Taman Bukul* and on the streets and parks of cities across Indonesia were the nights when any anxiety I had about making it through the trip or writing the book or what I would do when it was all over vanished. Steinbeck also said that journeys need a design, like everything else in the world, or the human mind rejects it and a purpose or the conscience shies away from it.[18] My design stretched from Aceh to Papua. My purpose was to take in everything I could that made Indonesia what it was. I never took in more than I did on those nights selling on the street.

***

I visit a few other interesting sights that are within a few hours of Surabaya. While I have already seen and climbed a number of volcanoes in Indonesia, Mount Bromo is in a league of its own. About an hour before sunrise, a local wearing a cowboy hat takes me by horseback from the nearest village to the foot of another volcano that looks out at Bromo in the distance. From there I climb to the top and watch the sun rise. The second part of the trip is to get to the top of Mount Bromo before the sun rises too high. Another cowboy gives me a ride on his horse and drops me outside a Hindu temple with a path behind it leading up the volcano. The area around Bromo is one of the last Hindu areas left in the country.

The walk up Bromo is much more intense than the walk up *Anak* Krakatau. That's because not only has Bromo experienced major eruptions within the past few months, it is experiencing minor eruptions this very morning. The soot from today's eruptions, yesterday's eruptions and who knows how many other eruptions is everywhere. This is not like stepping outside your front door to a soft three inches of snow. This is being caught knee deep in a raging blizzard. Luckily, I still I have my sweater since the air was chilly in the pre-dawn hours. I wrap the sweater around my head, breathe through it and look straight down to prevent the soot from flying into my eyes.

At the top of Mount Bromo there are a handful of other tourists. We poke our heads into the crater, but it is impossible to see very far. Every few minutes the gray cloud hovering about forty feet below us starts to rise simultaneously with a sound similar to fireworks. The cloud engulfs both our vision and our bodies. A minute later we can see again and we stick our heads back into Bromo and wait for the next eruption.

***

One night, P-Jax from Nusa Tenggara takes me to play basketball with his team. He says tonight is *And 1* night. I have a hunch what that means. While his friends are the most talented basketball players I have seen in Indonesia, *And 1* night, inspired by the films, is mostly one guy dribbling through his legs and around his back, desperately seeking an "Ohhh!" from the crowd, while eight guys stand at half court watching. There is actually a rule that you must always be within ten feet of the man you are guarding, which does not leave any way for the defense to end the nonsense. While the states can be proud of making basketball popular around the world, *And 1* might be my most despised American export.

As we are riding back to the loft on P-Jax's motorbike, he asks, "So, do you still want to see Doli while you are here?" Doli was after all, what I believed to be the most intriguing aspect of Surabaya before I arrived, but I was never actually in the mood to go. I figure if I do not go tonight I will never see it. After showering we are back on P-Jax's motorbike.

Doli is the largest red light district in Southeast Asia, which is saying a lot. A sprawling town of brothels

183

where all the men have apprehension in their eyes and the women seem to have given up on living a long time ago. I can count on one hand how many smiles, even fake ones, we receive in one hour of walking around.

We stop at a *warung* to get a drink. There are two girls sitting across from us who must be off duty. P-Jax asks if I want to go talk to them. I make eye contact with one of them. She looks me over, trying to figure out if I am going to waste her time. I tell P-Jax to forget it. Enough journalists, travel writers and bloggers have interviewed foreign prostitutes and framed it in their own way. I am not going to add anything new to this story. So we walk one more lap around and head back to the loft.

Prostitution exists all over the world, but what bothered me about it more in Indonesia was the hypocrisy that went with it. Karina lives in a neighborhood filled with college students, just a ten minute drive from Doli. Every night men, who are organized by a local strongman, part religious leader, part mobster, stand at checkpoints around her neighborhood. Young men and women are questioned and watched to see that no men enter the house of single women at night and vice versa. Karina has told me stories of these self-righteous vigilantes surrounding houses and threatening to kill young men unless they exited immediately. I would not be surprised if these same vigilantes were regulars at Doli.

I questioned Karina about what it was like to be a grown woman and treated like a child. She replied, "Here there are girls and there are married women. There is no such thing as a grown woman in Indonesia."

Back in Padang, my nightly walks home from *Pasar Seni* always included being honked at by a couple blue taxis that circled around the same quarter mile strip. A taxi would have two or three young prostitutes calling any men that passed. Most nights I would look straight ahead, knowing that the blue taxis would be discouraged and leave me alone quicker. But every once in a while I had to look. And there would be these young, pretty girls with tight tank-tops and way too much make-up looking at me with their well-rehearsed flirting poses, probably no more than fifteen years old. And I would walk the rest of those streets wondering how a city that takes so much pride in its Muslim faith could allow it.

One night I was drinking by the ocean with a group of foreigners that were working in Padang, when a crowd of men stormed the beach. These were not cops. They had no affiliation with the government. They were a volunteer moral police force. They brushed right past us and broke up into groups to attack each *warung* simultaneously. The owners of these *warungs* purposely leave the lights off at night because the only customers that stay after sunset are young couples looking to make out and possibly round second base.

The lights went on and terrified teenage eyes darted left and right looking in vain for a place to run. Some had to clumsily buckle their belts first. The army of hypocrites would then grab them roughly and toss them into a bus. They were taken somewhere to record their information, and their parents were called in to spread the humiliation over a whole family. The next day their names would be published in the local newspaper.

That night when I walked home down *Jalan* Diponegoro, there was no shortage of blue taxis honking at me.

***

I wait at the loft for Karina to finish her final exam. This exam has been postponed twice. The first time Karina received a text the morning of the test informing her. The second time there was a sign on the front door of her classroom. If you take a walk around an Indonesian university there is a good chance you will find a few dozen undergraduates hanging out outside of a classroom. Ask where their professor is and you will get comments like, "We don't know, but he/ she is very busy writing academic articles."

Many of these professors earned degrees in Australia, Europe and the United States. They have learned how to use multimedia and different teaching techniques to reach a classroom of students. However, when teaching, they revert to some of the most dated techniques such as standing in front of a classroom and paraphrasing a textbook. As V.S Naipul quoted a university administrator on his trip in 1980, "Some of them have been abroad, but there are many people whose bodies have been abroad but whose minds have stayed in the country. They remain villagers. They are there in the West only to get that diploma and to return to Indonesia with that ascriptive dignity."[19] Teaching methods aside, there are not many ways to deny a student the respect they deserve than not showing up for numerous classes and waiting until the day of a final exam to postpone it.

When Karina does show up, we each bring a small backpack and head to the bus station. We are setting out on a trip we have not planned very thoroughly. Karina is also a big fan of Pramoedya Anata Toer's writing. She is the first college student I have come across that has read his books. We set out for Blora, a regency of rice fields and the birthplace of the country's, if not the continent's, greatest writer.

We mention Blora to a few drivers at the bus station, and then we commit one of the deadliest travel mistakes. We put our trust in a very convincing ticket collector who says he will take us to Semarang, and that from there it will be a short bus ride to Blora. You can show up at most bus terminals and say you are going to Pluto and have every ticket collector swear that his bus goes there the fastest. After a four-hour bus ride to Semarang, in which we drive just north of Blora half way through the trip, we get on another bus and backtrack two hours, mostly through tranquil rice fields. We hop off in the town of Jetis and quickly learn that no one has ever heard of Pramoedya or knows where his childhood home is. Finally we find a *becak* driver who thinks he might know what we are talking about. He drives us just a few blocks down *Jalan Sumbawa* and lets us out. The gate is open, but there is no one around or even any proof that we are in the right place. After our greeting calls receive no response we walk through the gate and across a small yard. There is a one-story home with the windows open.

Through one of the windows I can make out a black and white picture of Pram wearing a farmer's cap and a poster that reads, *"Cerita dari Blora,"* (Tales from Blora) one of Pram's first collections of short stories. Karina and I are giddy with excitement, and I am too caught up in the moment to realize what big dorks we are.

Pram was born in this house in 1925. He left home as a young teenager and studied at the Radio Vocational School in Surabaya. He worked in a furniture store to help pay his tuition fees. He managed to graduate just before the Japanese invasion in 1942, which resulted in his next job being a typist for a Japanese newspaper. After Japan's surrender, when the Dutch tried to take back their colony, Pram joined a paramilitary group and wrote propaganda for the revolution's cause. He spent the last two years of the revolution in a Dutch prison.

Although Pram had a friendly relationship with President Sukarno, he remained a revolutionary at heart and was never afraid to criticize the new government's rampant corruption or its treatment of minority groups. Suharto's government had much less patience for a writer with communist convictions who had visited Russia and China and sympathized heavily with the plight of Chinese-Indonesians. During Suharto's genocide of communists and suspected communists, Pram was imprisoned on the remote island of Buru along with many other prisoners whom Suharto's regime preferred the Indonesian people forget. One of the greatest minds of the 20th Century spent the next 14 years (1965-1979) of his life doing hard manual labor.

The notebooks that filled his home were burned, his writings banned and as a prisoner he was not allowed a pencil or paper. But the injustices that Pram suffered only strengthened his resolve. During those years, as Pram was cut off from his wife, siblings, and children, often on the borderline of starvation, he created his masterpiece. Pram rehearsed his epic tale, which would later be broken up into four pieces of historical fiction, to his fellow prisoners. When after all those years he was finally given the opportunity to sit in front of a typewriter again, his 1,674-page Buru Quartet filled with ideal-driven characters representing the forces that created his country, was complete.

The central character of the quartet is Minke, a young, native Javanese man who grows up envying the advancement of European culture. His education, which comes from a wide range of viewpoints, pushes him to question colonialism and everything that is accepted by his people as the way of the world. Midway through the quartet, Minke dedicates his life to destroying this way of thinking and building a forum where Indonesian thought can flourish. Minke's character is loosely modeled after Tirto Adi Suryo, publisher and editor of Indonesia's first native-owned daily paper, but also draws heavily from experiences and lessons learned in Pramoedya's own life. What makes the Buru Quartet such a spellbinding, epic tale is that Minke is the symbol of the awakening and birth of a nation.

After his release, Pram spent another thirteen years under house arrest in Jakarta. His books were translated into English by the Australian Ambassador to Indonesia, Max Lane, an offense that cost him his job. The ban on these books was eventually removed, but Pram who died in 2006, was never given the recognition he deserved. He has received awards from institutions around the world, but many would claim that there was no Asian writer more deserving of a Nobel Prize. Regardless of awards or prizes, Pramoedya is not a household literary name, not even in his home country. I was shocked by the number of students and professors at Indonesian universities who either never heard of him or vaguely knew who he was.

After a few minutes of circling the grounds and reflecting on Pramoedya's life, we see an old couple approaching the house. With tanned skin, sleepy eyes and an innocent face that can only belong to one of the babies in a family, Sus Toer introduces himself and his wife. He invites us in, and we walk into a back room with walls covered in paintings and old pictures of Pram and other influential and artistic Indonesians. Sus Toer's wife brings us coffee and I explain what led us to his doorstep.

Sus was the sixth child born in his family. Pram was the oldest. Sus is also a writer and an intellectual. In 1963, Sus earned a scholarship to study economics in Russia. He claims to have learned the Russian language in three months and is still able to speak it, although I doubt he has many opportunities. He spent nine years studying and lecturing at a Moscow University. Also like his brother, Sus served his time as a political prisoner. Upon his arrival home in 1973, Sus Toer stepped off the plane at Jakarta's national airport and was immediately handcuffed. Suharto had been in power for almost a decade, but he was still not going to take any chances with communist indoctrinated minds roaming freely.

"I knew when I left Russia that I would face one of the three "B"s, *Bunuh* (killed) *Bui* (prison) or *Bebas* (freedom), and I knew the third choice was not likely. I was just lucky it was not *Bunuh.*"

"How long were you a prisoner for?"

"Five and a half years."

"Why did you leave Russia and place your life in Suharto's hands?"

"Because this is my country. I had to come home. Pram was very proud of me when he heard that I came home and survived those years in jail."

"Were you also imprisoned on Buru Island?"

"No, in Jakarta. But that's enough about that." It seems like Sus Toer does not want to dwell on the half a decade he spent as a political prisoner.

"One last question, why did Suharto set you free?"

"Because of your President Jimmy Carter. He threatened to embargo Indonesia unless all Communist prisoners were released. I am very grateful to Jimmy Carter."

That was a positive piece of American history I was not aware of. Making an enemy out of communists was a useful tool of tyrannies around the world. With military and financial support from the United States, dictators accused and locked up anyone who might pose a threat to their power of being communists. Carter is not an American president remembered for his strength in foreign policy. It was remarkable to hear that he was responsible for freeing thousands of communists and accused communists ten years before the Cold War ended.

Sitting there in that room with Sus Toer, with all of the pictures and books and living history around me,

I try to imagine these grounds in the 1930s with young Pram, Sus and their siblings running around. I also can not help but foolishly imagine that Minke, Pram's most noteworthy character had grown up here too, that this was where he had fallen in love with Annalies, first recognized injustice and grew a fierce pride in being a child of the Indies. Maybe the idea was not so foolish since Minke grew up in Pram's mind.

In 1942 Sus and Pram's mother died at the age of 37 giving birth to her ninth child. The child also died. In 1950, after the death of his father, Pram at the age of 25, came home to take his place as head of the house and ensure that the younger siblings were raised right.

"Pram could be very hard on us. He would tell me to come right home from school and do my homework. I didn't care about school. One night I came home late and he kicked me three times," Sus laments, almost looking to me for sympathy. I find it very endearing to hear an old man tell how his big brother, one of my favorite writers, kicked him when he was a boy.

"One day I was being naughty and Pram slapped me in the face. Later he and his wife picked me up in a *becak*. I sat in front of him and he put his arms around me and cried. He felt so bad for hitting me. Pram never once said he was sorry, but he had his own way of showing it. He took me to see a movie that night and then dinner, which of course was an expensive night for him." Pram's salary at the time was 180 rupiah per month (2 cents: Of course this was worth more before the Indonesian rupiah began to fall).

"Pram cried easily, but I always cried even more. Do you remember the boy that was always crying in Pram's story, *It's Not an All Night Fair?*"

"Yes, I do."

"He was writing about me. I cry often because it is good for me. It is good for my eyes. That is why I am 74 years old, and I can still read the newspaper without glasses."

Pak Sus offers for us to spend the night. He shows Karina to the guestroom, and he rolls out a mat on the floor of the main room for me. I drop my bag down and feel as if I am being given the nicest room in the White House. There is a *sate* place that Sus Toer wants to take us to. His wife does not like to leave the house at night, but like me, Sus loves walking at night. On the way out Pak Sus shows me his motorbike, which he has ridden all the way to Jogja 37 times already.

We go to a small open-air restaurant where the menu is fairly simple. We pick the meats that we like and the chef puts them on a grill in front of us and douses them with a brown, peanut sauce. *Pak* Sus keeps telling everyone that Karina and I are very rich people. He does not realize that Karina understands Javanese and is getting irritated.

We finish about thirty sticks of meat between the three of us. Before we leave, Karina and I take turns going to the bathroom, and *Pak* Sus tries to play Cupid. While I am in the bathroom *Pak* Sus tells Karina that I am a good man and that he can see in my eyes I will be a good writer and that she should make a move on me. When Karina is in the bathroom *Pak* Sus tells me what a beautiful, intelligent woman Karina is and that I should make my move.

The three of us need to walk off the *sate* so we head toward the main square. There is a park with children running around and adults sitting on benches.

"There must be a statue of Pram or at least a plaque somewhere, right?" I inquire.

"No."

"Nothing?"

"Many of the people here did their part in killing communists in the mid-1960s. They are not ready to recognize a man like Pram." More than 20,000 people were killed in the regency of Blora alone, mostly by their own neighbors.

"And besides the only book the people here think is worth reading is the Koran."

I doubt *Pak* Sus was ever able to make his peace with his country. Even after his release from prison he was still marked for the rest of his life. An extremely well-educated, worldly figure that spoke Russian and had experienced the world outside of these islands, Sus

Toer was banned from ever teaching in a university or anywhere else.

"When I was in Russia I would go abroad twice a year, sometimes for an academic conference and sometimes just on vacation. It has been a long time since I have been abroad."

Those days in Russia must have been the happiest of Sus Toer's life. An intellectual surrounded by other knowledge-thirsty colleagues, I imagine young Sus's eyes were opened to the wider world in a way he had never imagined, a world that his fellow countrymen would never understand. I am sure that he left an indelible image of Indonesia with those he befriended.

As we walk on there seems to be only one topic Pak Sus is in the mood to discuss – women.

"There was free sex in Russia. I imagine just like it is in your country, Kevin. As long as you did not get anyone pregnant, no one cared what you did. It was a very different way of living."

Pram was also a noted admirer of women. In the course of his masterpiece, the Buru Quartet, his protagonist, Minke, marries three different women, all of very different backgrounds, but each with a strength and fortitude that Pram must have first seen in his mother, who encouraged and financed his education. *Pak* Sus promises that before we leave, he will take us to the grave of Kartini, a Javanese writer who died at the age of 25 and is remembered as a pioneer in the

Indonesian women's rights movement. Kartini was also an influence in the creation of Pram's female characters.

I can not help but feel as if I am walking with Pram himself. After all, *Pak* Sus was a political prisoner, a writer, a man who was not afraid to step outside of the boundaries his society tried to establish for him. I have to remind myself before bringing the conversation back to Sus´s big brother, what a remarkable life he has lived, regardless of any family ties.

Sus continues to speak about the women in Russia, the ones that appreciated him and the ones that were too materialistic, the loves he left and loves that left him.

"There was this one gypsy I met in Moscow. We loved to walk around the city together and share our thoughts on love and life and many other things. She wanted to know everything about me and my country. It was almost time for me to come home, and I didn't want to leave her. I told her I loved her. I told her I wanted to spend my life with her and that when things were safe I would send for her. She said, 'I love you, but I can not live in your country.'"

I wonder if he had known for certain what the rest of his life would be like, if he still would have boarded that plane. It is not hard to imagine what *Pak* Sus thinks about when he sheds those tears each morning.

There is so much more I want to hear from Sus Toer, but I let my curiosity evaporate into the warm Blora sky. I can not not bring myself to make this old, gentle man answer my questions about prison life, his unfulfilled dreams and the big brother he misses dearly. So I let him go on about his gypsy love in Russia and the others that came and went along the way. I realize there is more truth in these forlorn tales of love than any historical conclusion I could ever make. There is a ray of enlightenment that shoots out from those sleepy eyes that experienced so much love and pain.

Pak Sus's door is open to anyone who wants to sit and talk with him. If you want to know more about the history of his family or the struggles he and his brother faced, just go to the town of Jetis in Blora and knock on the door of *Jalan* Sumbawa 40. But, I would not prod too hard. Because there is nothing that will open your eyes wider to what is good in this world than listening to an old man reminisce deeply into the rapture of his youth.

Toer House, Blora

Mount Bromo, East Java

Kantor Imigrasi
Bali

The Bali immigration office is tucked in on a quiet, tree-lined street behind the airport. I decide to just have a seat in the back for awhile, watch how the operation works and not make any sudden moves. There are about thirty people, half of them Indonesians, half foreigners sitting around. There appears to always be about five to eight *bules* walking around looking lost. The *bules* are mainly Australians. The men are all in shorts and tank tops. Some of the women are wearing bikini tops. I glance at my button down shirt and black pants. How could they possibly give me a hard time when I am the only one dressed for the occasion?

There are no instructions anywhere advising you where to begin your adventure. I learn from watching the other *bules* that you need to use your body as a peg and start at the back desk with *Bu*. As long as you do not piss *Bu* off, you get to jump three spots to one of the counters, each with a uniformed man behind it who has the authority to renew your visa. If you do happen to piss off *Bu* then you must take a seat and wait a sufficient amount of time before rolling the dice again. I am ready to play.

"Selamat pagi, Bu!"

"Selamat pagi." She looks over my passport, visa renewal application and sponsorship letter from the prince of Ternate. Without another word she points to Counter 1. I slide to the next box, wish the immigration official a *selamat pagi* and hand over my papers.

"Bhayu is the name of your sponsor?"

"Prince Bhayu, Yes, that's correct, *Bung.*"

He does not look impressed with the letter from Prince Bhayu, or the fact that I am wearing pants. "You can not renew this visa here. Bali is different from anywhere else in Indonesia. You can apply for a one-time 30-day tourist visa."

I am appalled at the idea of giving up my royal status, and if I settle for a tourist visa I will surely be forced to leave the country again in thirty days. "Excuse me, I was told that I could renew this visa anywhere in Indonesia. Maybe if you just called the prince that would clear things up." He hands me a tourist visa application and waves me off.

After going out to the parking lot for awhile to kick dirt and mumble Indonesian curses *"Anjing! Taik! Bangsat!"* (Dog! Bitch! Bedbug!), I return more composed with my completed peasant tourist visa in hand. This time *Bu* sends me to a different counter and official. The new official looks over my paperwork and addresses me, "Why did you fill out a tourist visa? You already have a renewable social/cultural visa from the prince of Ternate."

I glare over at the official at Counter 1, mimicking his words, "Because Bali is different." The dialogue continues running in my mind, "And as much as it would make sense for this country to have uniform regulations, instead of each island making up whatever asinine rules they want because they think they are special, I assumed the guy at the other counter knew what he was talking about. And by the way, I have seen monkey shit fights at the zoo more organized than this place."*

Even though I did not speak those last lines out loud I know this official has sensed the irritation and sarcasm in my voice. At this point it would not matter if I had come donned in robes from the wardrobe of Bali's first king. He is not going to help me.

After exchanging a few words in Balinese with the official at Counter 1, he hands my papers back to me. "I can't help you."

I stand helplessly for a few seconds trying to figure out which way to walk. My feet find their way back to *Bu's* desk. She refuses to accept my papers. I am not even allowed another turn to roll the dice.

I walk back toward the dirt outside. *"Anjing! Taik! Bangsat!"*

I take a seat on the steps and watch the big Australians dressed like they came to pick weeds

---

* I stole this line from the movie *The Replacements*.

walking out with their renewed visas in hand. They never taught at an Indonesian university. They have no ties to the prince of Ternate. They do not speak a word of Indonesian. Some of them barely speak discernible English. Yet they are walking out the door all smiles and "G'day mate."

I start daydreaming about how good it would feel to write a world renowned book on Indonesia. That someday two young female backpackers would be standing in frustration just where I was moments ago in front of *Bu's* desk, and one would yell out in despair, "And I thought Kevin Lee had a hard time renewing his visa." Her friend would laugh because she catches the reference, and so would a few other sophisticated tourists sitting in the room, and they would laugh too. And *Bu* and the other immigration officials at the counter would also get the reference, but they would not laugh because as soon as my book was read by the Indonesian Secretary of Transportation, they were all given a harsh tongue lashing and told they better get their act together. So *Bu* and the other officials would be reminded of that humiliating encounter and without hesitation knock off the nonsense and promptly renew those visas, much to the delight of those two sun-kissed, long-brown-haired, voluptuous beauties.*

---

* My email address is at the back of this book.

I thought I could handle a visa renewal in the most touristic part of the country, but after accepting failure I call my friend Jerry. He tells me he is on his way.

Jerry is a Batak living in Bali, who has a passion for flying small, remote control airplanes. He builds the planes himself and often takes road trips with his friends, driving hundreds of miles with their heads sticking out the window, watching their planes slice through clouds overhead.

Flying planes is what Jerry loves doing, but dealing with issues like the one I have today, is Jerry's expertise. His job title is *local partner*. When I asked him to expound more on what that meant he rattled off a number of businesses his foreign partners run from publishing houses to importing and exporting crafts. Jerry has no expertise in any of these areas, but still manages to impress these partners enough to stake a small claim in each business. Jerry is a lot like Winston Wolfe from *Pulp Fiction*. He is professional, efficient and helpful. Jerry solves problems.

If one of his foreign partners needs to buy a plot of land, Jerry makes sure that he gets a good deal. Trouble at the post office with a worker asking an outrageous price to ship a package, Jerry takes care of it. And if a bribe needs to be paid to make business run smoothly, Jerry deals with whomever needs to be paid and bargains a reasonable price.

Jerry is thirty minutes away when I call, but gets there in ten. I tell him the problem. He tells me to continue waiting outside. In the time it would take me just to get past *Bu*, Jerry is back. He needs 500,000 rupiah ($50), half of it for the social/cultural visa with royal status to be renewed and the other half for the "tip." I hand him the cash.

Two days later I return to Bali's *Kantor Imigrasi*, say as few words as possible and leave with another thirty days stamped on my passport.

8

Bali

In the mid-14th Century, Muslims began to push their Hindu neighbors east out of Java until Bali became the lone Hindu island of the archipelago. Today 80% of Indonesia's four million Hindus call Bali home.

Bali has opened her arms to tourists for decades. Beginning with people like K'tut Tantri, a woman from the British Isles who, having never found a place she felt truly at home, set sail for Bali in 1932. By her own account, as told in her autobiography *Revolt in Paradise*, she drove a car across Bali until it ran out of gas, which happened to be in front of the home of a *rajah*. The *rajah* adopted her as his own daughter, his fourth, and named her appropriately K'tut (K'tut means fourth in Balinese). K'tut dyed her red hair black, learned Bali's language, customs and art and grew a deep love for its people. She worked as a painter and opened up the first hotel in the Kuta Beach section, today by far the most densely tourist-packed part of

Indonesia. After the Japanese invaded, she assisted in the resistance, couriering messages and weapons across the islands, until she was captured, tortured and kept in solitary confinement for two years. After her release she befriended many of Indonesia's revolutionary leaders and played a pivotal role in Indonesia's quest for independence, convincing drunk European soldiers to share battle strategies with her and earning the nickname, Surabaya Sue, for broadcasting bi-weekly radio shows that expressed the Indonesian perspective to the English-speaking world.

While K'tut Tantri lived a remarkable life and there are many kernels of truth to be learned from her story, she has also been widely accused of gross embellishment and even her historian claims that she actually seemed amused when being called out on her fibs. "She set up a game. She would not volunteer what she considered to be 'untrue' in *Revolt in Paradise* but when I found evidence to suggest where she had dressed-up her past, she would sometimes admit it, usually with a chuckle."[20]

Just as K'tut Tantri's story holds some misleading anecdotes, for me the aura of Bali also possesses a bit more fiction than truth. The Kuta section is a sprawling abyss of souvenir shops, fast food restaurants and night clubs. Store owners stand in front of their shops trying to drag you in and hawkers shout at passing tourists offers of *ojek* rides and motorbike rentals during the day and ladies and drugs at night.

Bali is much more stringent in overseeing its cash flow than other islands are. My first and only day selling pearls in Bali, I teamed up with Wayan, a local who has a t-shirt stand on the beach. I promised him a cut of my sales, and since he had a vendor's license he promised to take care of any issues that might arise. When the police approached our table Wayan seemed to immediately find something irresistibly fascinating at the other side of the beach. Two uniformed cops waited for me to pack my things and a polite captain, who appeared impressed with my ability to speak Indonesian, told me with a warm smile that I can not sell merchandise without a license. I did not try to sell again in Bali.

***

After a few days I escape Kuta on a rented motorbike. I leave half my things at a hostel and with the other half on my back drive north toward Ubud. Ubud, the cultural capital of the island located in the mountains, has a cooler climate and more laid-back feel. There are plenty of temples and scenic gems within a short drive.

At the crack of dawn one morning I head out to a section of the island known for not burying their dead, but just laying them to rest in their forests. The next morning, I get some exercise by hiking a volcano, Mount Batur. My guide, Jai, is a short, pleasant man who is just as content to converse as he is to walk in silence. Both of his parents passed before his eighth birthday and he never attended a day of school in his life. He manages to provide a comfortable living for his wife and two daughters and has spent most of his life going up and down this mountain. Following his parents' death he began learning to speak English by selling bottles of Coke and Sprite to foreign tourists. Today he is known as one of Mount Batur's finest ambassadors.

Back at my hotel that night I read in a courtyard filled with Hindu shrines and stone water fountains. My room is immaculate with a marble floor, a private bathroom and a king-sized bed that when you lie on it, unlike most beds in Asia, actually gives a little. The woodwork on the exterior of my bungalow is decorated so intricately it looks like a mausoleum, in a non-creepy way. I can walk out through the doorway without ducking my head, to find bamboo chairs, and an always-full pot of hot tea.

There are many good reasons why Bali is able to hog most of the tourists passing through Indonesia, but I can not help myself from feeling irritated by all the comfort. Maybe if I was on a honeymoon I would appreciate the candlelit restaurants, the fresh pasta dishes and the hospitable service, but every bone in my body is itching to get back to what I consider the *real* Indonesia, with its screeching pre-dawn calls to prayer, cold bucket showers, mosquitoes and almost no one speaking English.

I ride back to Kuta and try to make a plan for the rest of my trip. Originally I had hoped to set foot on all eight major regions of Indonesia in the course of my journey, Sumatra, Java, Bali, Nusa Tengarra, Kalimantan, Sulawsi, Maluku and Papua. But after analyzing the amount of time and money I have, I can see that would be impossible. Nusa Tenggara, which completes the lower string of Indonesia's islands, is the first to go. Hundreds of islands that include the lesser visited paradises of Lombok and Flores, the self-contradicting West *Timor* (East) and the island of Komodo, which you can guess what it is famous for.

Back in Kuta I meet Brian, a backpacker from Northern Ireland who I end up drinking with for a string of nights. I forget all about making any more plans for my trip.

One night as we are drinking with two Argentine beauties and some Europeans from a cluster of different countries, the topic of traveling the United States comes up. Now, if someone gave you a few guesses as to what young tourists might find most memorable about their trip to the great United States of America I would imagine some reasonable guesses might be Times Square, Hollywood, the main drag of Las Vegas, the Northwest's national parks, the Grand Canyon or Bourbon Street. All would be wrong. There is one attraction that far outweighs any city or sight.

German: "Florida had the fattest people I have ever seen in my life!"

Frenchman: "No way, you can find human whales living in North Carolina."

Ukranian: "Louisiana is the fat hog capital of the world!"

Hot Argentine: "*Dios mío!* I thought the people in Boston were fat. Then I went into the countryside of Massachusetts. That's where you find the obese." All the guys nod their heads in agreement regardless of what they actually believe.

Slovenian: "I saw women with butt cheeks that would take up one bus seat each."

Frenchman: "I'm sorry, but you need to go to North Carolina. Then you will know."

Having stepped foot in 38 states I have a slight urge to set the record straight about where the fattest Americans call home, but feeling a little sympathetic toward my homeland I keep my mouth shut and wait for the argument to end.

Brian is a guitarist and singer. He seems to be traveling for inspiration and not to check off a list of places. He has a magical phrase, which he uses to excuse, forgive and let go of anything foolish he may have done, is doing or will do in the future.

"No helmet? Happy Days!"

"We used to put a bunch of darts in the middle of the living room. Then on my brother's call we would all run in, grab them and as we retreated, start winging them at each other. Kieran went to the hospital a couple times. Happy Days!"

"Another round of shots? Happy Days!"

"I think I'm going to call that really crazy girl we met at the bar last night. . . No, she wasn't that crazy. Why not? Happy Days!"

We have more than our share of Happy Days. I wake up late one morning and realize that my days and money are running out, and while the rest of this country has begun fasting for Ramadan, I am living in tourist central doing nothing to help my understanding of Indonesia. Another region gets knocked off my itinerary out of necessity. Kalimantan, which takes up most of the island of Borneo, one of the most exotic wildlife places on earth where you are encouraged to rent clubhouses high in the trees and an array of monkey families drop in to meet their new neighbors throughout the day.

I was once up close with orangutans (originally an Indonesian word meaning forest person, *Orang*: person, *Hutan*: forest) in Sumatra. I was feeding bananas, one niblet at a time to a female orangutan, who could have knocked me out with one punch. Becoming frustrated that I would not just hand over her entire meal, she lunged toward my backpack on the ground. Luckily, my tour guide had his share of experiences watching orangutans swinging from trees in mocking amusement as they waved wallets, passports, fanny packs and inhalers at *Orang Amerika* and *Orang Australi* below. He grabbed a hold of my bag just in time and suggested I quit provoking her.

Later I inquired if my tour guide had ever been in an actual fight with an orangutan.

"Many."

"How did that work out for you?"

"Win some. Lose some."

So, Kalimantan and more encounters of being outsmarted and most likely catching a beating from orangutans was out. Then after some more deliberation I conceded Sulawesi too. The oddest-shaped island on earth, resembling an undiscovered species of dinosaur. This island's snout contains quiet beach towns rumored to be filled with the most beautiful women in Indonesia. On its left knee, a region where Torajans save up for years in order to throw some of the most extravagant funeral ceremonies known to Man. And on its left foot, Makassar, where historically the Burgis sailors considered the art of boat-making so serious that after teaching their offspring the family trade they would abandon their young on a deserted island. If the boys wished to return to civilization, they had better have paid attention when *Pak* was explaining tricks on how to prevent boat leaks. The Burgis have such a bad-ass demeanor that the phrase 'boogey man' actually comes from the nickname given to them by European sailors.

After having to accept that my journey across Indonesia would take me through only five of its eight major regions, I bought a ticket for Ambon in the Muluku Islands. I had wanted to avoid flying for both poetic and logistical reasons. I wanted to say that I had made it across Indonesia's 3,200 plus miles by bus, train and ship, but backtracking all the way to Surabaya to catch a ship would waste too much time.

Another reason to avoid flying was my last experience on a national carrier, Lion Air. When I arrived in Aceh on a Lion Air flight to begin my trip, I noticed that everything in the top compartment of my checked backpack was gone. The missing items included vitamins, electronic chargers, batteries, a jump rope and surely other things I could not recall. When I went to file a complaint the next day with Lion Air, I was told I should have checked my bag at the conveyer belt before leaving the airport, as if every passenger is expected to empty their bags and check every item they packed on an airport floor. After a lot of complaining on my part to different Lion Air representatives, I was informed that I was welcome to fly back to the city I departed from and file a complaint there. Since Lion Air would not even give me the satisfaction of filing a complaint, Lion Air gets this paragraph in my book instead, and a reminder to readers to Google numerous articles on Lion Air's pilots and crystal meth. One was arrested just three months after my trip for almost half an ounce of possession and testing positive hours before a flight.

***

By my last night in Bali, Brian has taken off, and I am left to revel in the island's debauchery alone. After leaving a bar at around 2am, I am assaulted by the usual hawkers.

"Transport! Ladies! Mushrooms! Marijuana!"

I have had more than I can take of these guys so I devise a plan to annoy them as much as they annoy every tourist on the island. I wait for each group of foreigners to walk out of a bar or club and catch them first with my own calls of, "Transport! Ladies! Mushrooms! Marijuaaaana!"

They scurry away, trying not to make eye contact. I run along their side and delve into a rant of Indonesian gibberish until they finally turn to see who is speaking to them.

After about an hour and a half of my shenanigans I have a crowd watching me along with the irate hawkers that would rival Times Square's Naked Cowboy. I hear a young Australian, who I can not for the life of me remember talking to, shout, "I can't wait to read this guy's book!"

One of the hawkers approaches me slyly and says that the cops are walking around, and that if I really must keep this going I can yell, "Transport and Ladies," but not "Mushrooms and Marijuana." I tell him that then it wouldn't be funny anymore.

"Transport!   Ladies!   Mushrooms! MARIJUANAAAAAAAAA!!!!!"

One scowling hawker starts waving an empty beer bottle in my direction. His buddy is eying me and making a slicing motion at his throat. I figure it is time to call it a night and get some sleep before my flight.

Happy Days!

9

Ambon

My flight to Ambon went smoothly. I had a comfortable seat with a little extra leg room in an emergency row, a courtesy sometimes given to us fat Americans. I slept well and everything I put in my bag was still there when the plane landed. My good friend, captain in the Indonesian army and prince of Ternate, Bhayu, was at the airport to pick me up.

A couple hours later I am sitting on the floor of military barracks in the center of Ambon's downtown listening to Captain Bhayu whine about the recent weather. He goes on and on about how cold it has been, the dampness left behind from the rains and the chilling breezes that whisk off Ambon Bay and leave him and all his fellow soldiers with nagging, chronic colds. I can not help but laugh looking at these young, chisel-bodied soldiers sniffling and nursing their colds as they play video games. It is about 90 degrees out right now. The temperature never drops much below 70 degrees and the rains usually do not last more than a couple hours. I goaded Bhayu that I hope the Indonesian Army never has to fight a ground war in a Siberian winter. A couple days later I am also nursing a cold.

Since a foreign civilian lodging on Indonesia's army barracks long-term is out of the question, Bhayu promises to take me to look at a couple apartments in town. My plan for Ambon is to split one month between living in a Muslim neighborhood and a Christian one. Less than a decade ago these two groups went to war with each other. People that for hundreds of years had gotten along as well as any two different nationalities in a New York City neighborhood, watched their tropical island explode in bloodshed. Between 1999 and 2002, all over Ambon and the surrounding Maluku islands, mixed neighborhoods segregated, houses, churches and mosques were burnt to the ground, thousands were killed and hundreds of thousands were displaced.

Ambon was the first place in Indonesia where I spent a significant amount of time, and I had already made some good friends there in 2009. They were Christians that had their own families. They showered me with such hospitality and graciousness on my first trip to Ambon that I knew I had to delay contacting them. If they knew I was planning to live in a Muslim section of the island for two weeks they would have a heart attack. As I waited in the barracks for Bhayu to take me apartment hunting I started to reminisce about my arrival in Ambon almost two years earlier.

***

It was September of 2009 when I first arrived in Indonesia with the intention of living and working here for awhile. The plan was to spend a couple months not travelling, but semi-settled in a few places and then decide where I would live and what I would do. The search ended at Andalas University in Padang, Sumatra, but it started when I met two girls outside of an Indomart convenience store on *Jalan* Jaksa in Jakarta.

After a full day of flipping through travel guides, I found Prelly, a Chinese-Indonesian, and Jenny, a Batak, who were willing to have a drink with me and give me some tips on how to survive in Indonesia. I walked them to a bar where they were meeting a group of friends that all played in different bands together. A few of them spoke and understood a bit of English. Jenny spoke English well, but since she was never serious, it was hard to tell if her translating was meant to inform me or just confuse me more. Prelly, who spoke no English, said very little, even when Jenny offered to translate.

Over the next couple days Prelly, Jenny and other band members took me to a few sights in Jakarta. Prelly drove everywhere. Jenny and I would talk. I asked Jenny why Jakarta was so dirty. She casually teased, "Because there are so many Chinese." Jenny blamed everything on the Chinese. Prelly, whose father is of Chinese descent, glared at Jenny and muttered an insult about the drunken Bataks.

At some point I decided that Ambon would be my next stop. Prelly offered to drive me to the airport, and Jenny came along for the ride. I said my goodbyes to these two sweet girls, one whom I had gotten to know fairly well and one who was sweet enough to drive me everywhere. Before I walked to my gate Prelly asked Jenny to translate something for her. Jenny then informed me that Prelly's parents live on *Pulau* Ambon, and they would be at the airport to pick me up.

When I landed at 6:00 a.m., sure enough there was a Maluku woman, Mama Jo, and a round-faced Chinese-Indonesian man, *Pak* Robert, there to greet me. We shook hands, said "Prelly" a few times and threw my bags in the trunk. Prelly's cousin, Grace and her husband Kenny also came along for the ride. Grace was an English teacher at an elementary school. On the way to town, Kenny pointed out buildings that Muslims burned down during the recent *Troubles*.

Pak Robert was driving, and I was given the seat up front with him. Prelly's Dad looked as Chinese as a Terra-Cotta Warrior. Having recently lived in China for two years and in that time learning a few dozen phrases, I broke out my best *Bahasa Cina* (Chinese language).

"Nihao ma?" (How are you?)

Blank stare.

"Ni Shi nali ren?" (Where are you from?)

Irritated stare.

I put two and two together and realized he did not speak any Chinese. Grace offered to translate my English into Indonesian.

"Have you ever been to China?"

Grace translated.

"No."

"Was it your father that was from China, or your grandfather, or. . ."

A lot of words were translated.

Shoulder shrug.

"Do you follow what goes on in China? Do you have any desire to visit?"

Grace translated.

"No. No."

I leave the Great Wall pictures in my pocket, and we did not speak to each other for the rest of the drive to their house. For the rest of the day I met people that knew Prelly.

I met Prelly's cousin, Luku.

Prelly's aunts.

Prelly's Uncle John.

Prelly's little cousins.

Prelly's nephew, Nafa.

More of Prelly's cousins.

Prelly's nephew's babysitter.

Prelly's cousin's motorbike driver Oppie.

The guy who played the drums in Prelly's band when Prelly came home.

The introductions went well. I tried to remember as many names as I could. I was introduced as "Prelly's friend." They were introduced as "Prelly's (insert relation to Prelly)." They said "Prelly." I said "Prelly." We all said "Prelly." Smiled. Laughed. Basked in the multi-cultural experience. Once in a while a relative of Prelly would put their hand very close to their heart and lovingly say, "Prelly." I would respond by putting my hand even closer to my heart and lovingly saying "Prelly."

After finishing a delicious meal prepared by Mama Joe and her sisters, Prelly's cousins asked me where I wanted to stay while I was in the Maluku Islands. I told them my criteria, no more than $5 per night, quiet, near the beach. They pointed on my map to places in the center of the city.

"I don't think I want to be right in the city, maybe a more remote part of the island."

Everyone started speaking Indonesia quickly.

"No."

I was a little taken aback.

"What do you mean, no?"

"Because then we will not be close by when you need us."

I let out a deep sigh and realized that after all my talk about going somewhere exotic and starting a life for myself that I had allowed myself to be legally adopted by Prelly's family.

They made some phone calls, and drove me to my new apartment. It was a clean room in the middle of a downtown Christian neighborhood with a view of the Maluku Governor's mansion. I had no choice but to take it.

Mama Jo emptied a bag she had packed for me on the table, one plate, one knife, one spoon, one glass, tea bags, sugar, biscuits, butter, crackers, corned beef, 2 uncut loaves of bread, pineapple jam. When she pulled out the Skippy peanut butter I felt like hugging her. She continued pulling out a bed sheet, a blanket, a welcome mat, a big bucket so I could flush my toilet. Grace and Mama Jo spread a sheet across my bed, and then suddenly there was confusion on everyone's face. A lot of Indonesian was spoken. Grace flipped through my phrase book.

"Pillow."

We all looked at the bed.

I agreed. *"Tidak* (no) pillow."

After getting settled in, Mama Jo drove me to see their cousin who was visiting from Holland. We turned off on to a dirt path and pulled up to a house right on the beach. It was almost sundown and the view of the ocean was breathtaking. Mama Jo introduced me to her cousin, Uncle Timmy. I put my hand on my heart and started doing my Prelly routine until I realized that Uncle Timmy spoke English. He offered me a beer, and we sat and drank on his terrace.

Uncle Timmy was born in Ambon, but moved to Holland when he was two. He returned to Indonesia for the first time in 1982 and has spent every vacation since right at that beach house. After the initial introductory questions and some kind words about Prelly, Uncle Timmy, Mamma Joe and a few visiting neighbors forgot about me and talked amongst themselves. I was happy to sit in a water tube on the floor, listening, drinking *Bintang*, eating peanuts and watching the Banda Sea, content that although with no credit to myself, I already had my own apartment in town.

I read the few pages of my travel book on *Pulau* Ambon. I learned that for a small island in Western

Indonesia, Ambon held its own in the history department. Ambon was one of the original Spice Islands. The desperate search for wealth, European colonialism and even Columbus' discovery of the Americas (he was only trying to find a quicker way to get here), were all a result of the cloves and nutmegs that originated in Ambon and its neighboring islands.

One section of Ambon's history really jumped out at me. After World War II, Indonesia's independence from the Dutch appeared inevitable. Christians from Ambon and the surrounding Maluku Islands, dreading rule from a Muslim government in Jakarta, claimed the *Republik Maluku Seletan* (The Republic of Southern Maluku: RMS). They, like so many other people of Indonesia, wanted their own country. They fought, and like all their other Indonesian neighbors (except East Timor), lost.

Historically Moluccans held a close relationship with their colonial rulers. Many served in the Royal Netherlands Indies Army. Fearing that many people from these islands would be massacred, the Dutch stepped in and "temporarily settled" 12,000 Moluccans in Holland. Today there are over 40,000 descendants of the Maluku Islands living in Holland.

I waved Uncle Timmy to sit next to me and pointed to the paragraph in my book. He smiled, "Yeah, I'm one of them."

Uncle Timmy's father fought for the RMS. In 1951, when Timmy was two years old, they fled to

Holland. He waited 31 years before returning. He likes living in Holland, but said that the Dutch never really accepted them. To this day they are not allowed to join the Dutch army or vote in elections.

I tell Uncle Timmy about my trip through Tibet in the summer of '08, and how many Tibetans had given up the dream of independence, knowing that China and the balance of power in the world will never allow it to happen. Today most Tibetans only challenge Beijing on the issues that they believe are achievable, freedoms such as the right to choose their own Dali Lama and to teach the Tibetan language and history. I asked if the RMS has evolved into something similar. Uncle Timmy smiled.

"No. The Maluku Islands will gain their independence."

It was the first of many times in Indonesia that someone would tell me that the piece of globe I was standing on would be painted a different color some day.

"You really think the Maluku Islands will gain their independence?"

"It is inevitable."

Uncle Timmy went back to sit with his friends. He was obviously not going to share the RMS military strategy with a *bule* who just arrived that day and could not even find his own pillow.

By the time the sun dropped into the Banda Sea that evening, we were all toasting the RMS. When our drinks were finished, Mama Joe drove me back to my new apartment. For those first three weeks that I lived in Indonesia and to this day, Prelly's family looked over me like an adopted son, and Ambon remained a special place for me.

***

Back to my current trip in 2011, Bhayu is taking me around apartments in the center of town close to the island's main mosque, Masjid Raya al-Fatah. They look fine, but I can not get myself excited about being in the middle of this city. It is remarkable how an island so blessed with natural beauty can have sections like this. The streets are dark and drab, lined with dull buildings. The midday heat is magnified off the concrete and the stares of people in the street hold a tense severity as if the next war is just around the corner.

I spend another night at the barracks. The next day while Bhayu is in training I hop on his motorbike and drive toward Natsepa Beach. To get out of the city you have to drive through the street market that runs in every direction from the bus terminal. Traffic is always jam-packed with motorbikes and the stench of fish. Cheap plastic toys, home appliances and pirated DVDs are sold here. It is also the place where the conflict started. The account of how it happened has variations, often dependant on the religion of the person telling the story.

229

There was a disagreement between a Christian *angkut* driver and two young Muslim passengers on January 19, 1999. Christians say that two Muslims threatened the driver with a knife and demanded money. Muslims claim that the Muslim boys were collecting for a man the Christian driver owed money to. Regardless of the facts surrounding the initial disagreement, violence spread like wildfire across Ambon and its neighboring islands. By the following nightfall both Christian and Muslim homes had been burned to the ground. By the time the conflict simmered down more than three years later, at least 6,000 people were killed and 700,000 were displaced from their homes.

Members of the military and police forces played obvious roles of aiding one group or another from blatant inaction to weapon sales to actually taking up arms in the struggle. One catalyst that both Muslim and Christians I spoke with agreed on is that outsiders with their own agendas played a large role in instigating and prolonging the conflict. In the chaos that ensued following President Suharto's forced resignation, radical Islamist groups like *Laskar Jihad* (Warriors of Jihad) sought to cleanse Indonesia of any non-Muslims. Signs hung openly in Solo, Central Java calling for jihadists to get on a ship to Ambon and join the holy war. These ships set sail uninhibited.

In early reports of the violence, people who had lived in Ambon their entire lives claimed they did not recognize the men leading the mobs. In one torching of a Christian neighborhood, mob leaders cried for vengeance for the burning of *Mesjid Bawah Merah* (Under Red Mosque), though the mosque had not been touched. Once the initial fires were set, Ambon was turned upside down. With no apparent rule of land in place, many locals believed it was their duty to take up arms.

As I leave the city on a single main road that hugs the sea, I am always driving through either a Christian or a Muslim area. Crosses in one neighborhood and young girls covering their hair with *jilbabs* in another. In the early morning, Ambon's beaches are inundated with water. At Natsepa Beach waves pound the concrete walls, but by noon the Banda Sea retreats enough so that the children of the families selling *rujuk* can play in the sand. I pull over at a harbor just a few miles past Natsepa Beach and a crowd of men surround me. Everyone starts asking questions simultaneously.

"Mau kemana?" (Where are you going?)

"Dari Mana?" (Where are you from?)

"Lingap di mana?" (Where are you staying?)

An old man, Jalee, speaks to me slowly. I tell him I am looking to rent a room in the neighborhood. He hops on my motorbike and we drive one minute down the road to a family house with a five-room guesthouse extension. I meet *Ibu* Ga, a short, kind-faced woman who shows me a clean, dark room with a bed, chair, small coffee table and a tiny bathroom with a squat toilet and bucket shower. It goes for 50,000 ($5) a night, but she offers to make it 300,000 ($30) per week. Outside of the city, across the street from the harbor, walking distance to restaurants and a short motorbike ride from some beautiful beaches. I hand the money over and head back to town to grab my bag.

Driving back to town I am so damn proud of myself for finding my own place that I cruise right past the security check points, straight on to the military grounds. Soldiers start screaming, some with weapons in hand, and I brake to a screeching halt. After saying *ma'af* (sorry) repeatedly, they allow me in to get my things. I put my backpack on my shoulders, a book-bag in between my legs and take off.

Ramadan has begun, and Muslims all over the world are fasting from sunrise to sunset. I pass many crowded concession stands selling homemade cookies and cakes, which locals like to break their fast with.

Back at the hotel there is a cute, college-aged girl putting the finishing touches on my room. I go to introduce myself to her.

"Saya Kevin."

Before I can even put my hand out a guy with a Muslim cap and a long Taliban-like beard comes rushing over. Uh-oh. Maybe this was not the best place to rent.

He loudly introduces himself as Azhar. His wife is *Ibu* Ga's sister. He asks me the usual questions, and I respond with my usual answers,

"*Amerika.*"

"Taught English in Padang. Right now I am traveling across the country."

"Twenty-nine years old."

Azhar responds, "*Masih mudah.*" (Still young.)

"*Makasih, dan Pak?*" (Thank you, and you?)

"Fifty-two."

"You're still young too. You would look even younger if it wasn't for the beard."

"Yes, I know, but this is part of my identity."

"Of course." I feel bad because he may think I was insulting his beard.

"Would you like to join us for the break fast?" It takes me a second to catch on to the two-word phrase "break fast," and I accept.

"Great, I just need to shave first."

"Let it grow. A beard would look good on you."

I laugh and ask if I can borrow a mirror. In Java I became accustomed to shaving outside on my motorbike because it was the only place that had a mirror, but my bike here in Ambon somehow lost both rearview mirrors. Azhar asks around and returns with a broken shard of a mirror with six sharp corners.

The absence of a safe mirror reminds me of an American friend who traveled to neighboring Sulawesi in the 1980s. He went into the interior with a translator and befriended two primitive men that had been friends since they were children. When he returned from town days later he gave the men pictures he had taken of them. Each of the men roared laughing when he saw his friend's image trapped on a piece of glossy paper, but when looking at his own image asked, *"Siapa yang itu?"* (Who's that?)

We can hear the prayers being chanted from the nearby mosque as we begin to eat. The table is full of different dishes with a stack of fish in the middle. I am half-way finished eating before I realize that the seat they gave me is at the head of the table. Azhar and his wife are seated on opposite ends from *Ibu* Ga and her husband. Three boys and three girls aged nine to nineteen fill in the rest of the table. After tasting *Ibu* Ga's cooking I am certain I picked the right place.

The conversation is way more rambunctious than I would have pictured at a Ramadan break fast. *Ibu* Ga's sister is telling me about an American who married a woman in her family and lives somewhere on the island. One of the daughters, after hearing that I lived in China, starts spouting out every word she knows in Chinese. She is actually speaking Japanese. The fifteen-year-old girl talks about her basketball team and offers me a marriage proposal. And Azhar, the only one speaking English, is rapping away about his hippie days traveling around America's west coast and Asia.

"My Mom took my passport away and forbid me from travelling again. I waited a little while out of respect, and then I had to snatch it back. But, today I can't travel America. They see this beard and there will be problems."

"I understand, it's embarrassing."

"Yes, very embarrassing."

He thinks I was referring to him, but I actually mean it is embarrassing for me as an American to know how much a long beard can scare people. And it is sad to know that when I try to describe this jolly man, saying he has a Taliban beard is the best way I know how.

He drifts between English and Indonesian, never slowing down his spirited pace. After hearing where I began this trip he articulates his thoughts on why the marijuana in Aceh is the best in the world.

"We used to stuff our pillows with Acehnese weed and feel them get just a little more deflated each night as we trekked through Asia."

The bustling at the dinner table continues a bit longer as I go back to answering everyone else's questions. After dinner I read an English-Indonesian book with the younger children. By nightfall I feel completely at home in a neighborhood I never could have entered less than a decade ago.

***

Azhar and I quickly become friends. The more I hang out with him, the more childlike he seems, like an overgrown teenager trapped in a six-foot-three, 260 pound frame with a six-inch long tin-colored beard. One morning, after a late night of drinking coffee and listening to Azhar drift back and forth between his two favorite subjects, Muhammad and his younger days on the road, I hear his heavy footsteps getting closer to my door.

"Kevin! Still sleep?"

"Yes!"

"OK, continue!"

I continue for another three hours. When I join him at the dining room table he is antsy and looks like he has been waiting eagerly for me to come out and play. His wife makes us breakfast and tea. Whenever I attempt to clear the table or wash my own cup she has a hissy fit.

I feel comfortable sharing with Azhar my questions and qualms with Islam and organized religion in general. He has a sharp mind to compliment his eloquence. He listens intently, and offers responses grounded in the Koran. However, he does not waste much time debating doctrine. Instead, he fluidly shifts into stories, real life stories about Muhammad. About how he was always eager to serve, even in the simplest manners, like gathering fire wood for a feast or fetching water for his camel. He tells of the great compassion Muhammad felt for all human beings, and how to the surprise of his followers he once wept openly at the funeral of a Jewish man. He refers to Muhammad less like a prophet and more like a beloved uncle.

He is critical of his fellow Muslims. "The Saudis have had all this oil for so long. Why don't they learn something about it? All they know how to do is sell it."

He does not approve of the way Muslim girls in Ambon dress, how despite covering all their skin, except their face and hands, they still show off every curve of their bodies with tight outfits. Sometimes he loses me, like when he says that one of the reasons polygamy is acceptable is because there are four times as many women in the world as men. "Just look how many women are in this neighborhood."

Azhar always loved to read, especially about America. He rails about the indignities committed against the Cherokees and the determination and guts of the Wright Brothers. Unfortunately, like many of his fellow countrymen, Azhar has a recurrent explanation for the causes of many of the world's ills.

"Ahhh, the Jews. They run the Democratic Party in your country. They run Bush's party too. Look at the Cold War. It was completely made up by the Jews. They created communism. They created capitalism. They pull the puppet hands all over the world."

Azhar does at least wrap up these rants on a slightly more positive note. "Brilliant people those Jews. Who else do you know that could pull that off?"

And as serious as this man can be – with a forehead that is permanently discolored a dark ash from decades of pressing his head to the floor in prayer – he can just as easily shift a conversation about his beloved prophet back to his careless hippie road trips. One trip was his six-month journey down North America's west coast from the fishing town in Alaska, where a boat dropped him and a friend off, all the way to Mexico's Baja Peninsula.

"Ohhhh! (clenching the hair on his head) Those senoritas! I was a real hippie. I loved walking those streets in California, listening to the way your black people talk, 'Yo Man, Yo Man. You want to get high.' Yes Sir, we did!"

Azhar starts rocking his head back and forth with an imaginary joint in his hand and then puts his nose to the table and takers a long sniff with each nostril to help me picture the scene.

"By the time we got to San Francisco we had no money. We had to go to this church that was promoting some new religion. They were all Japanese. We didn't understand any of it, but we prayed and smiled and said yes to everything they preached, so they would give us food."

"Do you ever feel guilty about any of it?"

"Noooo! What would be the point in that?" I guess Islam does not hold guilt up on the same pedestal Catholics do.

Azhar closes his eyes and tilts his head back. It seems he wants to relive his younger days in his mind a little longer as he bobs his head and strokes his beard, singing to himself Bob Marley's *Buffalo Soldier*.

Sometimes the women in the house come by and demand that Azhar tell them what he is rambling on about. Azhar answers them with a thick American accent in a language they do not understand, "Maybe yes. Maybe no. Maybe rain. Maybe snow."

After listening to a few of Azhar's morning stories I am usually starving. This is my second Ramadan in Indonesia. My first year I briefly considered taking part in the fast as a way of connecting myself to the people here. After some reflection I decided that I enjoyed eating too much, and that not eating or drinking anything from sunrise to sunset in 90-degree weather was just not a hardship I wanted my body to endure. So I made up my own fast that I felt would show some respect toward my neighbors while not forcing myself to look like Alexander Supertramp at the end of *Into the Wild*. I would wake up before dawn to eat my breakfast, and then allow myself nothing but fruit and water until the sun dropped. I kept this up for three weeks, engulfing four bananas and two apples each afternoon with the door to my visiting professor's office closed before giving up. I could see that no one really had any respect for my attempt to feel connected. After describing my self-fitted fast, my neighbors would proceed to tell me that their 9-year-old daughter could do the real fast with no problem, pointing to a girl sitting on a plastic stool with misery written all over her face. I eventually realized that even if I could endure a proper Muslim fast it would still not earn me any fans. Their fasting had a purpose behind it. It showed their love of Allah and their willpower to follow Muhammad's example. Fasting was one of the greatest gifts they give to Allah each year. An entire fasting month made them distinct from believers of any other religion. My attempt, as a non-Muslim, to take part in their fast seemed as pointless to them as a man who tries to gain weight to feel connected with his pregnant wife.

I ask Azhar if he would mind very much if I ate a sandwich in front of him. "Of course not." I start slicing up the apples and smoothing my peanut butter on white bread.

"Are you sure you don't mind?"

"No. Maybe if you were cutting up a fat piece of lamb my mouth would water, but you can eat as much of your American Apple Pie as you want. It won't bother me."

Although Azhar and I disagree often, I come to admire him deeply, less for his wisdom, as for the way he acquired it, leaving his home to seek truth and for his non-forceful, yet passionate way of passing on that wisdom.

"How did you manage to pay for all your travels?"

"Like you, Kevin, I brought things with me from home and picked up clothes from the Salvation Army. Then I sold whatever I could on the streets."

Azhar takes a deep puff of his cigarette and goes back to singing *Buffalo Soldier.*

***

Ramadan comes to an end on *Hari Raya Idul Fitri.* I start the day by going to the mosque with Azhar to pray. All of the standing, kneeling and prostrating gives my legs a good workout. It also gives me a special feeling hearing the prayers chanted and just being surrounded by people who are so happy to celebrate such an anticipated day for reasons both religious (the strengthening of the bond between the individual and Allah) and practical (they can finally eat during the day again). *Ibu* Ga has all of her kids impeccably dressed, her daughters in white dresses and her sons in slacks and golf shirts. Azhar stays home with his wife and father-in-law to relax and greet friends who will be stopping by, celebrating the most important day of the year. *Hari Raya Idul Fitri* appears to be an all day marathon of racing from house to house and wishing as many relatives, neighbors and friends a *Selamat Hari Raya Idul Fitri* (Happy Idul Fitri Holiday), while stuffing your stomach with *kue* (cake). Nevertheless, I do sincerely appreciate *Ibu* Ga taking me along and introducing me to everyone as if I were one of her children. I pass out as soon as we get home that night.

The next morning as I am eating my "American Apple Pie," Azhar tells me we need to walk down the road to meet someone. I grab my bag and follow him. Boys are running around with plastic guns, which appear to be the number one toy bought with *Idul Fitri* money.

Another favorite toy to buy with *Idul Fitri* money is counterfeit Indonesian bills. For 1,000 rupiah (10 cents) you can get 1 million fake rupiah (fake $100). The children buy a pack of play money, which looks exactly like Indonesian money, only slightly smaller with a plastic feel. They sit outside and mimic what the grown men do at night time, gambling over games of dominos. Azhar spent the morning gambling with a group of young boys on the corner. As we pass the children, Azhar's provokes them by stretching his wide shoulders back, causing his belly to protrude a little more, and proudly removing his prayer cap to show off all the fake Indonesian rupiah he won. Some of the bills twirl off Azhar's head like leaves from a tree. He clumsily snatches up the brightly colored bills and plops his stuffed cap back on his head. He lets out a jolly laugh and loudly exclaims that these young kids need a lot more practice. The incensed kids, who would probably jump Azhar if he did not outweigh each of them by 200 pounds, pretend to ignore him.

We enter the house of Azhar's friend, *Pak* Ali, a fisherman. Ali was witness to a piece of Ambon's history that I am interested in. In March of 1957, military and civilian leaders in Manado, Sulawesi formed *Permesta* (short for "Universal Struggle Charter"), another link in the long chain of rebel movements in Indonesia's short history. One year later *Permesta* announced its support for the PRRI (Revolutionary Government of the Republic of Indonesia) in West Sumatra, linking these two different groups and giving Jakarta two simultaneous headaches to deal with on each side of the country. *Permesta*, which drew support from parts of Sulawesi and the Maluku Islands including Ambon, was formed because of the same underlying reason as West Sumatra's rebellion; Jakarta was stifling their regional development and hurting their economy. They were fed up with Javanese rule.

As the separatist revolution in West Sumatra was already under way with heavy CIA support, the CIA wasted no time in supporting another large scale operation that if successful might help a small piece of Indonesia break away and become a staunch ally of the US. Sukarno's talk of a non-aligned movement during the Cold War era was becoming too much for US policy makers.

Prior to Mao and the Communists' ascent to power, large areas of China were filled with minority groups that did not hold any allegiance to Beijing. Some policy makers believed that instead of backing a losing horse, the Kuomintang, the US should have concentrated its powers on breaking up China so that when the Communists won the war, their empire at least would not have stretched as far as Tibet or Xinjiang. President Eisenhower, weary of a neutral Indonesia in the Cold War world, did not want to repeat President Truman's perceived mistake.

The CIA began sending sanitized planes over Ambon on strafing missions to assist guerrilla operations there. I start to ask *Pak* Ali, who I am sure already assumes I am with the CIA, some questions about the rebellion.

"Did the majority of people on Ambon support *Permesta?*"

"No, there were some Christians and Muslims who gave their support. Most people here in Ambon wanted nothing to do with a civil war."

"What was your opinion of the US at the time?" He stares at me for a few seconds. "They were the enemy. They were bombing us."

"Right, of course." I clumsily look back at my notes and try to make sure my next question is not a dumb one.

"Can you describe what those days were like when Ambon was being bombed?"

"Before the first planes flew over Ambon, my teacher told me to go home and build a bunker. He did not say why. We did not use any light or fire at night. We thought it would make the chances of our homes being bombed less likely. There were three straight Sunday mornings that we were woken by war planes overhead. Early one Sunday morning, a low flying plane bombed an oil tanker. My uncle was working the docks that day and was killed. I was just 16 at the time. All of my classmates and everyone in town knew the US was assisting the rebels."

The Indonesian government claimed that 700 of its people were killed on that one day alone. The American public was left in the dark on what was happening in Ambon. In early 1958, Secretary of State John Foster Dulles addressed the rebellion in a testimony before congress, "We are not intervening in the internal affairs of this country." Following a public accusation by President Sukarno of American bombers and pilots being used in attacks, President Eisenhower responded in an early May press conference, "Our policy is one of careful neutrality and proper deportment all the way through so as not to be taking sides where it is none of our business." The New York Times strongly backed these claims, "The United States is not ready . . . to step in to help overthrow a constituted government. Those are the hard facts. Jakarta does not help its case, here by ignoring them."[21]

On May 18, 1958 Allen Poe, a pilot from Florida, was flying a bombing mission over Ambon when his plane was shot down. Poe parachuted into a coconut tree and was captured by Indonesian soldiers. It was protocol for all CIA-operated planes to be sanitized of any link to the U.S. Fully aware that he would have little chance of survival as a stateless person, Poe secretly packed about thirty incriminating identification items leaving no question that he was a pilot for both the US Air Force and a CIA-operated airline. Poe served four years in prison before Sukarno released him. His plane crash marked an embarrassing moment in America's involvement in Indonesia.

I ask *Pak* Ali if he could write his full name down for me. He looks around the room. I tell him if he prefers, I will not use it in the book. He begs me not to use his name. He also will not let me take his picture. Azhar and the other men jibe him, "Stop being such a little girl!" He still refuses and says he is afraid the CIA will come after him.

Ali, his friends and I talk about broader topics for awhile. He asks about Obama and seems to have a strong curiosity in American presidents. He mentions President Kennedy, who actually agreed to accept President Sukarno's invitation to visit Indonesia just three days prior to his assassination in Dallas.

"Whatever happened to your President Kennedy? Who killed him?"

"No one really knows. The government claimed that Lee Harvey Oswald shot Kennedy and was acting alone. Most Americans believe there is much more to the story."

Azhar sits up as if abruptly waking from a dream, "I can tell you right now who killed Kennedy. The Jews!"

Pak Ali and his friend look to me for confirmation. I shake my head to at least show my objection. It is too early in the morning to argue with Azhar.

I can hear Azhar muttering into his beard, "Such brilliant people those Jews."

***

A few days after *Idul Fitri*, the town of Mamala holds their annual *Pukul Sapu* (Beating Brooms) festival. The main event is when a group of about forty Muslim men take turns whipping each other bloody with palm sticks. The ceremony is believed by locals to be a sacrifice to Allah and a prayer for the health of Ambon's people in the year ahead. Azhar does not approve of the festival. "It misses the point. Muhammad never asked us to hurt our bodies in that way."

Prince Bhayu picks me up and we drive on his motorbike over the island's main mountain to Ambon's northern shores. When we get to a town called Hitu, we stop in front of a house on a quiet block that is surrounded by an iron gate crowned with fleur-de-lis. Bhayu says he has to run in to use the bathroom. I ask him who lives here. He responds coolly, "The King of Hitu." I tell him in America, we usually stop to take a leak at gas stations or 7-Eleven's.

I briefly meet the King of Hitu, a pleasant guy in his mid-30s, and we continue on our way to the festival. In the first act, children of all ages do little dances or show off their martial arts moves. Bhayu says it is very traditional. Then a band starts playing. There is a woman in her thirties, dressed in jeans and a tight t-shirt singing and shaking her hips like a Salsa dancer. There is also an old guy on stage with a mohawk that plays the fool chasing her around, trying to get a feel of her little body. She puts on a show, drifting between light flirting and slapping him away when he gets too fresh. Eventually she pretends to push him, and he tumbles down a flight of stairs to the eruption of laughter of at least a thousand people present. I assume that this is also a traditional Muslim act.

At about 5:30, an hour before sundown, which takes place at pretty much the same time all year across the country, the action is ready to start. Drums begin beating louder and louder. A group of men, women and children with faces painted black walk out first. For me, this is the tensest part of the ceremony, much worse than the actual whipping. I think back to when I attended *Pukul Sapu* two years earlier. A bare-chested man with a hanging belly led the opening procession holding the hand of a little girl about seven years old. The girl was wearing a shirt tucked in that must have been five sizes too big for her. The face on her shirt was Osama bin Laden's. Fortunately, this year there is no bin Laden shirt.

The men, women and children pray together. Some of the children cry. The drum beating gets louder. Soldiers stand around the perimeter of the field, some holding AK-47s. Every one's eyes are fixed on the men who will momentarily be sacrificing their bodies for the health of the rest of us. The men range from short and skinny, to muscular, to tall and overweight. They are all shirtless with red shorts.

And then it begins. The sounds of vicious gusts of wind exploding on contact fill the arena. Each man paired up with another pulls a thin palm tree stick from the batch in his hand and whips his partner with all his strength. The one being whipped takes a couple steps back in between each whip. After he has backed up the length of the field it is his turn to do the whipping, and his partner retreats in the opposite direction. Every one likes to claim that the men do not feel any pain because they are in a deep trance. I look at their faces. At least some of them are feeling it. The welts expand and protrude from their chests and backs. Their bodies are a bloody mess that you would only see in a movie about slavery or torture. Yet they continue the dance, whipping, being whipped, trading pain and welts, offering their sacrifice up to Allah.

After a few times back and forth the twenty or so men take a break and another paired group steps up. The two groups rotate a few times until each group goes for one last whipping finale. A few of them look scared and in pain, but most of their faces just look serene and proud.

One short man, who must be at least a decade older than any other man out there, seems angry that no one is hitting him hard enough. He screams at his partner and every one else. He screams at the crowd. When he passes by, he is a few feet from me and I can feel the surge of wind from his stick. He has more welts and bigger welts on his body than any of the other men.

The whole ritual lasts less than ten minutes. When it is over every one in the stadium exhales. The fans walk onto the field. I shake hands with a few of the participants and they look at me with relaxed smiles, as if they just finished a light jog. Eventually the bloodied men all go to the stands where old women begin rubbing coconut oil on their body. Bhayu and I do not want to get caught at the back of this long traffic line that will surely fill the narrow road leaving Mamala. We race ahead, and after a quick bite to eat at the king of Hitu's house, we are back on the road.

They say that within a few hours all of the wounds will be healed by the town's special coconut oils, and any trace of Mamala's sacrifice will have disappeared. Apparently once every four years there is an even more intense ceremony on another Maluku island, where Muslim men really crucify each other by stabbing one another and cutting tongues off with swords. Azhar and Bhayu both insist that it is real and that the wounds incurred are also completely healed. Although Azhar says they use black magic and that again, they are missing the point.

Bhayu is a one of the strongest defenders of mysticism I have met. That night while we eat on the outdoor terrace of Café Panorama, I ask Bhayu why he stood so far back during the *Pukul Sapu* ceremony and did not join me up front. "I did not want my powers to interfere with theirs and cause them to feel pain."

I laugh and Bhayu smiles, but I know that he is serious when speaking about the powers of mysticism, especially those regarding his kingdom. I ask him to tell me all of the mystical stories surrounding his island of Ternate.

He tells about the snake who bit off a man's head and now speaks Javanese. The snake told Bhayu and others that were in the palace to inform the Sultan he should not break from traditional practices. There was the boat trip Bhayu took with the King of Tidore when a crocodile appeared and pulled their ship ashore. Then there is the Sultan's crown, which contains hair from every Sultan of Ternate dating back to 1257. The hair still grows at such a rapid pace that it needs to be cut regularly. Once a scientist attempted to experiment on the crown, but was mysteriously hurled backwards as if he had been kicked.

While Bhayu seems to get a kick out of people from the Western world not believing any of these stories, he does not revel in the enchanted details. Instead he uses these legends to communicate lessons about his kingdom that he believes hold significant truth. Unfortunately I am usually too dumbfounded with trivial questions about the snake and crocodile to catch any of these truths.

Bhayu was actually born to a Javanese king. At a young age he was sent to Ternate to become the fourth son of their Sultan. Bhayu says that it is good for royal blood to mix. In 2010 I visited Ternate, but unfortunately Bhayu was tied up with his military engagements and could not be my tour guide. The Sultan's Palace was a large, but unimpressive structure in the middle of the downtown area. Since the Sultan today does not hold any political power it was difficult to place exactly what kind of prestige being "The Prince of Ternate" held. In American terms I would rank it somewhere above a city councilman, but below a star high school quarterback.

Every time I brought up the Sultanate to locals they were able to recite the names and details of the present royal family, including the adopted son from Java. However, my revelation that the Prince was my good friend did not result in any comped drinks or render anyone speechless.

Bhayu and I have plenty to talk about outside of kingdoms and mysticism. He tells stories about the year he spent in North Carolina on a military exchange program. The soldiers on their nights off would go out to the bars and embellish their foreign friend's royal blood line in attempts to get everyone laid. Bhayu is also an aspiring singer and has already created an album. As much pride as he takes in his kingdom and his country, he also seems ready to escape it and see more of the world.

We share a lot of laughs late into the night. When I get back to my room, I watch the videos of *Pukul Sapu* on my camera over and over, which I am sure would have outdone any of SportsCenter's top 10 plays of the night.

***

I spend the next two weeks in a Christian neighborhood closer to town with Prelly's parents. Mama Joe is as hospitable as ever. She and her sisters clear out a spacious room that opens up to a large open-air rooftop terrace looking out all the way to Ambon Bay. There is always plenty of fried rice, eggs, beef and chicken, and Mama Joe makes sure that there is always a canteen of hot water with plenty of tea and coffee on hand. Most days I take an *angkut* ride with Prelly's cousin, Nahru, to Natsepa Beach where I sell my pearls and stones and talk to locals.

Pak Robert and I are able to communicate much better this trip, and I do not repeat the mistake of inundating him questions about his Chinese ancestry. Some nights a couple dozen friends and family members gather on the rooftop. While they sing Jesus songs, *Pak* Robert and I escape toward the back where we can talk about politics, business and those years that ripped Ambon apart. The market where all the violence began on that tragic January afternoon is just a short walk from his home. He turns so that we are both looking down on the town. Not far from the coast the land elevates and anyone who lives on the island can tell you which patches of hills are Christian neighborhoods and which are Muslim. He waves his hand over the land, *"Semua ini terbakar."* (All this was burning.)

Although the home we are in is not in a completely homogeneous Christian neighborhood, *Pak* Robert does not fear his neighbors. "That war was not started by Ambon Christians or Ambon Muslims. It was started by outsiders. It was started over politics. They just used religion as their tool."

In Michael Vatikiotis' haunting story, *The Spice Garden,* he evokes the mood, violence and devastating remnants left behind by the Maluku conflict on his fictional island called Noli. A Muslim merchant and a Christian priest work together to end the bloodshed as a Muslim boy and a Christian girl run away so they are not pulled into the hatred that has engulfed their families. Vatikiotis reminds his readers that fear is the driving force behind violence. In one conversation the merchant reminisces to the priest, "It was like this before, you know, when the army came looking for the communists. Once the violence erupted, people believed that carrying dismembered digits – noses, ears and even genitalia – protected them from bullets, spears and arrows." In an early scene of the book a local of Noli, overhearing of the bloodshed in Ambon, laments, "God help us if this ever reaches Noli. Our children are innocent and know nothing of prejudice."

Remembering trips to Ambon and Sulawesi two years earlier reminds me how many of my best times in Indonesia were spent with members of Prelly's family. Prelly's cousin Grace and her husband Kenny are one couple I feel lucky to have met. We hang out randomly, usually on short invitations from Grace. One day Grace took me on a hike up to a cliff overlooking the bay, where we saw a large, obscure "Hollywood" sign. Another night Kenny and I attended the annual *LA Lights Jazz Festival*, where we listened to bands ranging from blond-haired Europeans singing in Arabic to a young Indonesian rap group with a lead singer that looked ten months pregnant.

Another night Kenny and Grace take me to the bar at the Amboina Hotel. Kenny introduces me to four men seated together at a back table. They smoke and smoke and drink a lot of juice. Billy, their friend and fellow brass band musician is on stage singing. He insists that I get up and sing. I insist that I do not because I can not sing, do not like singing and no one in this room would ever want to hear me sing. Billy walks up to the microphone and introduces me. I down my *Bintang* and reluctantly join him on stage. I make him stay up there with me, and we sing "Stand by Me." There is no recording of the song, just one keyboard player playing from memory. He seems to struggle to keep the music in tune with my singing. At the end every one gives a very half-hearted applause, much less enthusiastic than the applause I received when I walked on stage.

To resurrect the mood of the night, Kenny and Grace hop on stage. Kenny is on the keyboard and Grace sings in English and Indonesian. Both, in their early 40s and married fifteen years, they seem like their only care in the world is showing me a good time. Kenny, who has a small frame and dons a heavy, push-broom mustache across his beaming smile, reminds me of a darker Cheech Marin. By the middle of their first song, the whole bar is smiling with Kenny, and the damage I caused has been fixed.

Billy and his friends tell me how much they admire the "old nigger singers" from America. I try to correct them, "You mean Black singers?" They frown. "Yeah, yeah, nigger singers." None of them are the slightest bit racist, and some of them are only a few shades lighter than Miles Davis himself. They talk about Miles Davis and Louie Armstrong and other Jazz greats I have never heard of. They say that the Dutch songs are terrible, and the only good English bands are the Beatles and the Stones, "but those old nigger singers are the best." I think if Louie Armstrong walked into the bar right now they would all drop to their knees and tell him he's the best old nigger singer they ever heard.

*****

I go with Grace one day to the grade school she teaches at. The students look happy in their blue bottom and white top uniforms. I play a few games with them to practice their English. I read them *Anak Berani*

(The Brave Kid) in English and Indonesian. They all laugh at my pronunciation of their language. When it is really bad they correct me. When the story is finished I tell them that I am like Gaga, the brave boy in the story, because even though my *Bahasa* Indonesian is terrible, I am not afraid to stand in front of them and practice. I tell them that they speak English much better than I speak their language, and that if they want to speak English well they must be *berani*.

I hang out in the administration office with Grace, the headmaster and a few teachers. Kenny is in the middle of playing the keyboard for a college graduation next door. As the graduates names are read, he takes a break to hang out with us. He starts telling me what an amazing cook the headmaster is. *Bu* Yetti smiles and seems quite satisfied with the compliment. Kenny continues to feverishly compliment the headmaster, and describes certain dishes that she has cooked in detail. Eventually I catch on to what Kenny is doing. A few more flattering words and we all have a dinner invitation to the headmaster's house later that week.

Kenny and Grace send a motorbike driver to pick me up. I hop on the back and the driver hands me a thin plastic helmet that looks and feels like a larger version of the plastic baseball caps I ate ice cream from as a kid at Yankee games. He drops me off at the headmaster's house. *Bu* Yetti has plenty of questions for me about teaching in China and other places I have travelled to. Grace and Kenny arrive shortly after with another teacher, Ulla.

I met Ulla after my lesson the week before. Ulla treated Grace and I to lunch at a small *warung* in the predominantly Christian neighborhood. Every meal on the menu included pork. When I ordered my fried rice without pork, the waiter said that it was impossible for them to cook it without pork. Since Muslims are banned from eating pork, it was a clever tactic by the owner to keep his clientele the way he wanted it without appearing overtly prejudiced.

Kenny was not kidding. We eat a tasty Sumatran dish with rice, chicken, strips of scrambled egg, burnt bread crumbs and plenty of spices. The headmaster carries herself in the same way principals I knew at home did, with her head up, seemingly ready to correct the slightest misbehavior at the drop of a hat.

A couple thin, light green geckos run around the walls. A dog walks in the door and under everyone's legs. I tell the headmaster she has a nice dog. She says she has no idea whose dog that is.

I hate to bring up a topic like Ambon's conflict while enjoying a good meal, but I can not help but feel eager to hear firsthand from Christians who lived through it. I try to bring it up casually, "What was it like around here during those years around 2000?"

Kenny jumps up. "I go out every day with my gun shooting them."

The homes of many of Kenny's relatives were burned down. Because it was not safe to stay in his own house he went to live in a refugee camp with them. The headmaster left Ambon to live on a safer island with some of her distant relatives. Schools closed down. Thousands of young boys, some as young as seven years old put down their toys and picked up Molotov cocktails. Torching schools, apartment complexes and places of worship became the primary duty of child soldiers.

Kenny says that the Indonesian Army treated the Christians like they were trespassing in their own land. Christians had more allies in the police force. Every house had guns ready to fire. I ask if the government collected the guns after the conflict ended. Kenny says everyone still has their guns hidden in their house.

When I spoke with Azhar and his brother-in-law about the "Troubles", they were just as critical of the forces that were supposed to protect the people of Ambon. They said that the military made a lot of money selling rice and weapons. The price of a bullet was never higher. One day a group of their neighbors decided they had suffered enough of the violence and perpetual fear. A few families packed their young and old into a small boat and in the middle of the night set sail for the island of Sapura. Without any police or military escort, the Muslim families hoped to reach land by dawn and find relatives there. Within an hour of their departure all nineteen were gunned down.

Ulla, a soft-hearted woman who loves filling up her Facebook page with pictures of flowers, had been quiet most of the night until now. "I was driving in to town one day with a Muslim friend. I needed to buy food and basic things for my family. There had been a lull in the violence, and I thought that in broad daylight we would be safe. We turned a bend in the road and there was a roadblock. We saw that it was Muslim men with guns. They were pulling Christian men, women and children out of their cars, blindfolding them and throwing them in a van. I quickly covered my hair with my friend's extra shawl. When we reached the checkpoint, I tried my best not to look afraid. He looked at me for what felt like an eternity. I said, 'Assalamu alaikum.' He waved us on with his gun."

Kenny is fired up. He curses the men who brought the war to his island and the ones who made life for him and his family miserable. I have heard him speak like this before, but never with so much rage. Then he tells me something that I was in no way and never could have been prepared to hear.

"My son was outside playing when they took him. . . He was only four years old. . .We didn't know where. . . didn't know if he was dead or alive. . . All we did was pray and search, pray and search. . . And then word came from town. . ."

Kenny makes a high pitched slicing sound and runs his thumb across his neck from one ear to the other.

My body goes limp. I wait for someone to tell me that I misunderstood, that somehow Kenny was trying

260

to express something else. That these two people who have treated me like family, who tell me what an honor it is to have me as a friend, who sing karaoke together as if they did not have a care in the world, that their son did not have his throat cut open at four years old.

I look at Grace. Her eyes are staring right through me.

"We didn't accept the news," Kenny continues, "We kept searching. Searching and praying. Searching and praying. We were on our own with no one to turn to. Eight days after he was captured, five days after we were told he was dead, rumors spread that our son and other boys were still alive and being held in a town called Sipur. Two days later the police, acting on a tip from a Muslim neighbor, raided a house in Sipur. That night our son was returned to us. . . He had been blindfolded for ten days. His body was unharmed, but he never fully recovered. He stays with family now on another island and is still traumatized."

Despite the far less tragic ending, I still feel sick to my stomach, and want to get up and go outside. Kenny senses my discomfort and gives me a big smile, the same smile he gave me when we first met, the smile he always gives when playing the keyboard. He outstretches his arms and says, "But now everything is OK."

***

Less than 48 hours after I leave Ambon the press releases read: "Riots broke out in Ambon on Sunday, claiming three lives and injuring 60 others. . . Three people were killed as police fired shots to stop the riots. They were identified as Sahrun Ely, Djefry Siahaan, and Cliford Belegur. Several cars were also set on fire. National Police spokesman Insp. Gen. Anton Bachrul Alam said police had deployed 200 mobile brigade forces from Makassar to Ambon to help safeguard the area and claimed that situation was under control as of Sunday evening. The riots broke out because of a rumor saying that Darmin Saiman, an *ojek* driver from Waihaong sub district, died of torture. . . The fact was he died from a single [traffic] accident as confirmed by an autopsy."[22]

The city is on lock down. Friends of mine who live close to the religious borders leave their homes to stay in "safer" parts of the island. Other friends post pleas on Facebook to "Pray for Ambon." The word Ambon is on the lips of all Indonesians who stay abreast of current events, uttered with a sigh of despair. The U.S. State Department issues a travel warning for Americans to avoid traveling to Ambon. The Jakarta Globe reports that a provocative text message had been circulating around Solo and other parts of East Java urging Muslims to go to Ambon to wage war. Two weeks later a suicide bomber enters a church in Solo and blows himself up. Indonesia is once again reminded that those who sow the seeds of hate still have a strong voice here.

Hundreds of miles away by now, I recalled a late night conversation with Azhar. I had just finished telling him about a scene I had witnessed earlier that day. I was inside of a home downtown, eating with a family when a fight broke out between two men in the alleyway outside. There was a lot of commotion, and then it quieted down. A few minutes later one of the men returned with a sword in his hand. He was promptly tackled by the majority of the neighborhood.

What troubled me most was not the fight, which could have happened anywhere, but the way people in the neighborhood reacted to it. Obviously having neighbors prevent the distraught man from using his sword was beneficial, but every man, woman and child seemed to feel an instinctive urge to be close to the skirmish. Young boys and girls stood just a couple arms length from the crazed scene. Not a single mother or father grabbed a kid or ordered one to get out of the way. I stood in the doorway and possibly from an impulse to do something manly, used my body to block three women and a few kids from going outside. They pushed me with all their might. Their screams merged with all the other sounds of mayhem outside, and I was not sure if they were directed at me.

After the clash ended and the tension had been deflated, the women acted as if nothing had happened. They went back to gossiping and laughing as if the entire scene was a soap opera they had just finished watching.

I conveyed all of this to Azhar that night. He looked at me in complete understanding. "Kevin, that's just the way it is here on Ambon. When the rains fall, the people run inside. When the bullets fly, they run outside."

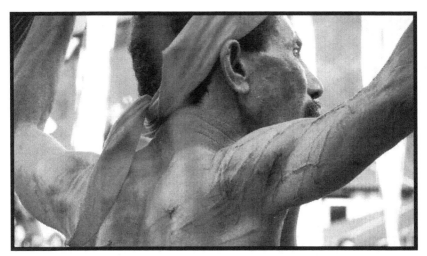

Mamala, Ambon

Mamala, Ambon

Tulehu, Ambon

Tulehu, Ambon

Mamala, Ambon

Tulehu, Ambon

Kantor Imigrasi

Ambon

An *ojek* driver drops me at the top of a hill, just outside of downtown. This is it. My last visa renewal, and an important one since it will be a long, expensive plane ride to Malaysia if they deport me.

Long pants: Check

Passport: Check

Bag of *"Bu"*s, *"Pak"*s, *"Bung"*s, *"Da"*s and other appropriate forms of address: Check

Money for Visa Renewal: Check

Money for "Tip": Check

Patience and reminder to self that procedures in other cultures do not always run smoothly or with any discernible logic: Check.

There is no one in the lobby and just a few female immigration officers in side offices. A plain, uniformed girl walks out and asks in English, "Can I help you?"

"Yes, I would like to renew my visa." I decide to save all the flattering commentary about her country and island.

She smiles, hands me a visa application renewal form and asks me to fill it out. After filling it out, I hand her my form and passport. "Please come back in two days to pick up your passport and renewed visa." I almost burst out laughing. Maybe this is her first day. Still I ask for her name, Ira, thinking maybe I can make a request to only deal with her if I run into problems later.

Two mornings later, I return and again cute, little adorable Ira is the one to greet me with a smiling, "*Apa Kabar?*" (How are you?)

"*Sehat.*" (Healthy)

Ira hands me a ticket, "Please go to the back counter to pay your visa fee." Near the bathrooms, there is an old man sitting behind a counter. I hand him the ticket and 250,000 rupiah ($25). He counts the money, stamps a receipt, hands in to me, nods and says, "*Terima Kasih.*" I would not be surprised if this was the only work he has to do today.

I walk back to Ira's office. She is at her computer, looking at pictures on Facebook. I stand in the doorway and wait for her to notice me. She jumps up smiling, looks at my receipt and hands me my passport. "Your 30-day visa renewal is inside. Enjoy your time in Indonesia."

I start looking up and around the room for candid cameras. I can just picture an old couple watching me on live TV. Their toothless mouths gaped open as they fall out of their seats laughing, "The dumb *bule* thinks they renewed his visa!"

I stand speechless, looking at my visa, almost sad. Maybe Ira needs someone to teach her how things work in an Indonesian *kantor imigrasi*. The interrogations, the bribes, the pointless questions, the lengthy bureaucratic procedures, the mind games that make you feel like you have committed unforgivable sins. Is she really going to let me walk out the door without even asking why my last name is Lee?

Ira seems to be getting nervous. I think she is coming up with excuses in case I ask her out. Instead, I ask if I can have my picture taken with her. An older, skeptical official snaps our photo, one that I am sure to reminisce over with my grandchildren some day.

I walk out the front door, and just like that, my visa renewal days are over.

Ambon

10

Papua

It was three days and three nights at sea from Ambon to Jayapura, the capital of Papua. At some point, shortly after departing we must have sailed by *Pulau* Run, an obscure island with a population of 1,000 that I had wanted, but never had the chance to step foot on. The British owned this island up until 1667 when the Dutch made the worst trade in world history, pre-Boston Red Sox. No money or future draft picks involved, just a straight up swap. The Dutch took *Pulau* Run and the British took an equally obscure island in the New World, *Pulau* Manhattan.

There was an excitement that came as my ship glided toward Papua that meant much more than just the conclusion to a trip. In America, we drive west for the cool air of the Rockies and the meditative vastness of deserts, forests, big skies and the Pacific. When the day comes that a cross-country trip is a requirement on the passage to Indonesian manhood, there is no question the road will lead east, away from the strict households of Sumatra, the politeness of Java and the Disneyland of Bali to one of the most exotic, untouched places on earth.

New Guinea is the second largest island in the world. An arbitrary line slices it in half. The eastern half, today called Papua New Guinea (PNG), had its days under the control of Germany, Britain and Australia before being granted independence in 1975. The western half of the island makes up Papua, one of Indonesia's largest and least densely populated regions. Indonesia's claim to Papua, lay in the assertion that any land that had fallen under Dutch rule was now Indonesia. After many years of debate and intervention by the United Nations, Papua was annexed by Indonesia in 1969.

Although the island may have officially belonged to European powers for hundreds of years, colonies and missionaries were concentrated in coastal areas, and most were short-lived ventures. "Up until the late nineteenth century, all New Guineans were non-literate, dependant on stone tools and not yet organized into states."[23] The majority of people on this land, about the size of Spain and Italy combined, lived in the interior, and well into the 20th century remained completely indifferent to the technological advances of mankind. To this day, many still are – roaming the jungles in tribes, hunting and gathering their own food.

The ship is not quite as long or tall as your average cruise ship, but definitely packs in more people. There are about eighty people in each low ceiling room with nothing but a few televisions and long rows of adjoined cots where everyone sleeps shoulder to shoulder. Luggage is kept under sleeping spaces. The lights remain on throughout the day and night. During the day those who do not have a clear view of a television often share cots with those who do. *Money Train* with Wesley Snipes and Woody Harrelson plays every day with Indonesian subtitles. In hallways, stairwells and even the outside deck, passengers sleep using their luggage as pillows.

As the only *bule* on the ship and naturally a local celebrity, I greet everyone in my sleeping area and tell them my story. There is a crew of boys, about ten years old, who say I look like one of their favorite soccer players, Cesc Fabregas. They wake me up most mornings so I can join them on their walks around the ship. I spend most of the three nights at sea on the upper deck canteen either reading about Papua or listening to stories from Papuans.

One night, four Papuan engineering students on their way home sit at my table. The three guys are all wearing straight brimmed baseball caps. We talk about simple things like the NBA and how when I was a kid, no one in my neighborhood would wear a cap until it spent at least one night being curved by a rubber band. Since I know I will only have so many chances to hear a Papuan's opinion, I ask, "Do you believe Papua should be independent of Indonesia?"

There is a long pause as the four of them stare at me. Victor, who is wearing an NYC cap, leans in toward me, "Yes Papua should be free." The sole female repeats Victor's words and the other two guys nod in agreement. While during my short time in Papua I would meet some who doubted the likelihood of Papua ever breaking away, I did not meet a single Papuan who believed Indonesia had any reasonable claim to their land.

Before the Dutch surrendered to Indonesia in 1949, they demanded a ten-year period to develop Papua in return for recognizing the new government in Jakarta. During this time the Dutch built schools and colleges that offered training in every field from carpentry to law. (For some reason they never thought of doing this during the first 350 years they were in Indonesia.) They also attempted and succeeded in inspiring an independence movement. In 1961, Papua raised its Morning Star flag, and plans were made for an official state to be declared in 1971.

The U.S. sponsored talks between the Netherlands and Indonesia in 1962. The New York Agreement awarded Indonesia control of Papua, but stipulated that an election on self-determination under UN supervision take place no later than 1969. Shortly after President Suharto's ascent to power, he earned some legitimacy when an American mining company, Freeport, became the first foreign company to sign a contract with his new government. Freeport was granted concessions to large swaths of land in Papua, without consent from a single Papuan. Today Freeport's mines in Papua reputedly hold the biggest reserves of copper and gold of any mines in the world. In the five years prior to my trip across Indonesia (2006-2010) Freeport paid approximately eight billion U.S. dollars in taxes to the Indonesian government.[24]

Following the New York Agreement, the Indonesian military moved in quickly and began a campaign of terror across Papua raping women, burning villages and murdering anyone suspected of supporting *OPM* (Indonesian acronym for Papua Freedom Movement). Amnesty International estimates that at least 100,000 Papuans have been killed by Indonesian forces since the 1960s. Over a six-week period in the summer of 1969, one of the most mystifying referendums in history took place. Just over 1,000 Papuans, handpicked by Jakarta, voted unanimously for Papua to become part of Indonesia. Although the referendum was supposedly supervised by the United Nations, rumors stand of electors being threatened at gunpoint, loaded with beer and injected with drugs. What makes the result even more baffling is that prominent members of the Papua Freedom Movement, such as Theys Eluay, casted their votes in support of inclusion. To this day Papuans demand the UN call for a new referendum on self-determination and for all Papuans to be given the right to vote.

There is a full moon illuminating the water below us, and a cool breeze has begun lapping the decks of the ship. "What will you do after you graduate from college?"

The lone female speaks up, "I will try to get a job with Freeport." The three guys say that Freeport will be the first place they apply for a job.

This is not the answer I was expecting. "But I thought you don't like Freeport?"

"We don't, but what else is there? We can get a starting salary of six million rupiah ($600) per month and possibly move up to twenty million ($2,000). And we want to stay connected to our land."

"It is sad, but today we need Freeport. We are so rich. We have all these natural resources, but we can not even dig them up ourselves."

"Papua is Indonesia's kitchen. Everything they need is cooked here. Maybe when Papua does become free, we will be in the right place to help it happen."

I look at each of them and ask, "How do you think it will happen?" No one is willing to take this question, but finally Victor speaks up, "It is only right that Papua be free. I believe it will happen."

A lap around the deck of the ship never fails to charm me. An old man tries selling me one of the Bibles out of his bag. "You know Billy Graham? I am Papua's Billy Graham." Another Papuan man with a tucked in button-down shirt and an air of success about him speaks about his twenty-three years working as a miner with Freeport, "It was hard work of course, but I did well for myself. I have a nice home. All three of my children went to university in Java. I never dreamed I could have afforded that."

The most entertaining time of day is when security does a quick, yet meticulous ticket check. Bathrooms are locked and everyone is asked to stay where they are with their tickets out. The teenage boys that snuck on without a ticket hide under blankets, in safety boats and behind families with tickets. Amazingly this under matched, out of shape security force is always able to round up a long line of at least twenty smirking culprits just in time to march them down the plank and leave them in the next town. Before their departure their eyes seem to flicker around the ship looking for a way out. It reminds me of prison tag, as if they are just waiting for someone to come slap their hand so they can run free.

When it is my time to walk down the plank and depart in Jayapura, I look around for Sarah, a Papuan woman about my age who I found through Couch Surfing. All I know about her is that she has a brother living in China, and that she is interested in learning to speak Chinese. I wonder if I will recognize her as the gigantic porters rush off, knocking my backpack around and me with it. A short woman, her hair in long thin braids looks up at me, "*Nihao?*" I look down at this girl, much less tribal than her picture led me to believe,

"Nihao." We walk together and switch to languages we can actually speak, first Indonesian, and eventually English since she is fluent, and I need a break.

She takes me to a house on a long narrow lake that once belonged to her grandfather. He was a village chief, which is a pretty big deal around here. Supposedly he helped a lot of locals out in his day and was very wise, even correctly predicting the hour of his death. I meet Sarah's aunts and little cousins. After a long, relaxing swim, we join her aunts on the deck in a boisterous card game. They are all chewing and spitting betel nut.

As I look around the room I have this deceiving feeling that I am surrounded by a familiar culture. Sarah, her aunts, the kids running around, everyone in the neighborhood is Black. I would not call them African-American because there is absolutely nothing African or American about them. According to Jared Diamond, one of the most renowned anthropologists of our time who happened to spend the better part of three decades on this island, Papuans and Aborigines are actually the original inhabitants of Indonesia and greater Southeast Asia. Approximately 40,000 years ago migrants from present-day China conquered almost the whole of Southeast Asia, causing Papuans and Aborigines to retreat and settle in isolation in their respective remote lands.

I had assumed that Papuans would not have been so different from their Asian neighbors with the exception of their skin tone. The first time I walked into a reggae club filled with Papuans, I saw how wrong I was. Most of the men were larger and more muscular. The women had fuller bodies and they all danced with a certain rhythm I have never seen among any other Asian group. Many of the men around Jayapura have long foreheads, thick beards and wide noses. Between the ship ride and the drive to the lake I have already spotted a couple Lebron James look-alikes.

I stay with Sarah at her house just outside of town. One of her aunts and a few young cousins are also temporarily staying with her. Not many Indonesians in their 20s can afford their own place, but Sarah is not your average Indonesian. She is one of the most business-savvy people I have ever met. Like my friend, Jerry in Bali, Sarah is the "local partner" in a variety of businesses in Java and Papua. Foreigners send her checks every month for using her name to do business and for sorting out the occasional government related issue. I am sure many Indonesians would give their last bowl of *nasi* for this job, but it takes someone with Sarah's English language skills, competence and trustworthiness.

Sarah has another exciting business where she journeys deep into the Papuan jungles to meet roaming tribes and trade with them. Often she returns with 24k gold. Freeport workers are not the only ones that know how to dig. She then sells this gold in town for a sweet profit. Sarah also takes plenty of charitable trips into the jungle where she brings vitamins and medicines that these tribes are in desperate need of.

Naturally, at first I question the truth of this cute girl with stories that make her sound like she has a heart and pockets of gold. It is not that I think she is lying. It is just that when someone comes from a culture where men predict the exact hour of their death, I wonder if their sense of reality can get a little muddled. However, after just a couple nights staying with Sarah I could see that there was nothing fake about her pockets or her heart.

Every morning Sarah has a healthy, delicious breakfast of eggs and vegetables cooked for me. Some days she goes to work in a government office. She says she has to have some tangible role in the community or she will be looked at as a witch. Other days she calls in sick and we bounce around town together. Every night someone comes by the house asking her for money. One evening I hear an aunt yelling at Sarah, "I don't need 800,000 ($80). I need one million ($100)!" Another night a cousin says he broke his helmet and needs to borrow hers. She tells him she does not want his big sweaty head in her helmet, but gives him 300,000 ($30) to buy a new one, which will definitely buy the best helmet in Papua. Another night her younger sister wants money for a flight to Sumatra to see her ex-boyfriend. While I am sure Sarah could afford the ticket, she consoles her instead and tells her it is not a good idea.

The night after her rude aunt leaves with Sarah's money, I ask her why she is so generous, even with people who do not seem to appreciate it. "It's just money. Here when people see you have something they expect you to share it."

Most Papuans are only a generation or two removed from living in small tribes. Survival of these tribes required that food, clothing and anything they came into possession of be shared equally. I recall a story where a foreigner gifted a local tribal leader with a short-wave radio. The old man stared at it for a long time and seemed irritated with being given a gift that seemed impossible to share equally with a hundred of his people.

***

Early on a Thursday morning I am sitting shotgun in a brand-spanking new, yellow Mitsubishi dump truck listening to a classic American mix tape filled with songs like *Love me Tender, Strangers in the Night* and *Unchained Melody*. Diang drives and I do my best to translate the words of Elvis, Sinatra and the Righteous Brothers into Indonesian. He has been listening to these songs all his life with a very vague idea of what the words mean. I met Diang last night on a walk around Sarah's neighborhood. He was playing cards outside a *warung* with some other non-Papuans from Sulawesi and Java. I mentioned that I would like to see the nearby city, Sentani, while I was in town, and Diang immediately offered to drop me off and take me home on his work route.

Diang and his wife are from Sulawesi. Their child was born here in Papua. They moved here a few years ago to take advantage of the economic opportunities. With all of the nickel, copper, gold, timber, rubber, petroleum, cocoa, tea and sugar on Papua's land, as well as the shrimp and tuna in its seas, it is easy to see why Papua is the "Kitchen of Indonesia." For Indonesians willing to move to Papua they can easily make three times what they would at home for similar work. Papua's vast land and resources relative to its tiny population make it an ideal spot for an opportunist willing to move to an obscure place. Papua accounts for 24% of Indonesia's land mass, but just 1.5% of its population. For your average Indonesian, taking a job in Papua is similar to an American taking a crab-fishing job in Alaska. And there is no doubt that working in Papua comes with its own catalog of dangers.

As we drive west on the only road connecting Papua's northern cities, the Pacific Ocean is off to our right, and the mountains to our left are the only barriers between us and the mythical Papuan jungle. A couple days earlier, a man walking on this road was speared by an arrow shot from these mountains. Tensions around Jayapura have been escalating recently as the fifty-year-old conflict reaches another boiling point. Less than two weeks prior to my arrival, a protest in Jayapura made headlines in the New York Times, "Thousands of people rallied for independence from

Indonesia in the country's Papua region on Tuesday, after days of political violence that killed at least twenty-one people."[25] Right in the center of Jayapura, a group of unidentified people armed with machetes attacked two minibuses killing four and wounding nine.[26]

Campaigning season for local government seats is in full swing. It must be difficult for Papuans to follow politics without the flames of *merdeka* (independence, freedom) being stoked. Election season seems to remind locals that Papuans living on the other half of their island have had their own independent nation since 1975, while the world seems indifferent to their own independence.

The Indonesian government restricts travel by foreigners to Papua. Journalists are banned from visiting Papua without special permission. My friends from Padang emailed me their doubts that I would be permitted entry with the current political climate. I imagined myself just like one of those ragged immigrants arriving at Ellis Island and being told to get back on the ship. Fortunately for me, if the government is barring entry to foreigners, they are only monitoring the airports.

Diang drops me off at a *warung* in the center of town and says he will pick me up at the same spot at 5:00 p.m. this evening. I take an *ojek* out to an area called Post *Tujuh* (Seven), a neighborhood of *bules* that have lived in Papua for decades. My driver points to a few houses where missionaries, teachers, translators and pilots live. We spot a middle-aged American man in shorts and a white t-shirt taking his garbage out. I introduce myself and mention that I am hoping to learn more about Papua. He invites me into his house.

Raffy and his wife are missionaries. They are also gracious hosts with a deep understanding of Papua's people and a strong will to aid their advancement. He says Papuans share everything to a fault. "Often family members of my gardener show up expecting to be handed part of his paycheck." He says that Papuans do not have much of a work ethic because the one who works the hardest does not end up with any more than the one who works the least. Naturally outsiders from other Indonesian islands come here and take the best jobs.

Raffy says he understands the fairness ingrained in the concept of the hardest worker being given a job, but he sympathizes with these Papuans who have to settle for the most menial jobs in their own land. It is as if they have just overnight been pulled from the Stone Age and are scrambling to make it in the Facebook Age. While Raffy's first aim might be to bring Christ to the Papuans, after hearing of all the educational programs he assists, I can see he is also preparing them for today's world.

Christianity may have come late to Papua, but it came with full force. I am amazed each night, as I sell my pearls on the main street of Sarah's neighborhood, how many people use the Bible to explain and defend everything they do. It is the same mentality I see in the book I am reading, *The Testimony Project: Papua*, where twelve Papuans, most of them leaders in their respective communities, testify to the troubles of their people. Papuans both in the book and on the street give their own interpretation of *Romans: 13* or the Old Testament prophet, Amos, to justify why they are taking a stand against rule from Jakarta.

There are certainly primitive Papuan beliefs that the arrival of Christianity has helped diminish, such as the voluntary cutting off of fingers and ears to show grief for deceased relatives. But there are other shifts in thinking that if Papuans from a few generations back could witness, they would slap their Christian offspring upside their heads. Like when someone quotes Jesus' miracles of multiplying three loaves and two fish or catching a few hundred fish in one cast of his net as models to grow their economy. Or quoting *Luke 4:18* to justify fighting for their freedom, or even worse not fighting back against injustice because "it was Sunday"[27]

As Benny Giay, a leading figure today in the Free Papua Movement, stated, "The church there [in Papua] is the only agent through which people there can know the world."[28] It is sad for me to hear that all of the wisdom and courage earned and passed down over thousands of years to guide Papuan life is being thrown away and replaced by one book. I wonder if their unquestioned obedience to Christianity lies more in their desire to enter the New Age or to highlight the contrast between them and their Muslim occupiers.

I thank Raffy and his wife for their hospitality and find my way back to the main road. My *Lonely Planet* makes note of the most provocatively named site I have ever heard of, *The Papua Freedom and Human Rights Abuses Memorial Park.* I ask for directions from a few people in town. They look at me as if I just walked into a black tie dinner and asked, "Where's the shitter?" I suppose with tensions being as high as they are, "Papua *Merdeka,*" is not a phrase you use lightly with strangers.

Not a single local or *pendatang* (outsider) is able to point me in the right direction. Eventually I am able to use the *Lonely Planet* map to find a field overtaken by knee-high weeds and plastic garbage. It appears to be the most abandoned plot of land on Sentani's main road. In the middle of the field is a tin awning held up by wooden stilts over a square block of concrete, large enough to shield maybe a dozen people from the harsh sun. I sit down by myself next to Theys Eluay's gravestone, painted in the Papuan flag's blue and white stripes and read my book.

Theys Eluay is the most recognized figure in the Free Papua Movement. As equally controversial as he was charismatic, Eluay donned a white afro and a white beard, making him look like an edgier version of Fredrick Douglas. He was the head of the Papuan Presidium Council, which worked to democratically achieve independence. He was also known to hold close ties with Indonesia's military command in Papua and was rumored to have used them to put out hits on his own people.

On November 10, 2001 Theys Eluay was dragged from his car and strangled by *Kopassus*, a U.S. trained Indonesian Special Forces unit. This is the same Special Forces unit that in 2013 stormed a prison in Java, killed four inmates and later admitted to it. None of the soldiers responsible for Theys Eluay's death were given more than a three-and-half-year jail sentence and some still hold important military posts on other islands. For many Papuans, Theys Eluay's murder exemplifies the oppression they live under.

About an hour and a half later the memorial welcomes another visitor. A lean Papuan wearing a backwards baseball cap sits next to me. I hope that he has come to pay his respects to the most noteworthy figure in his region's long struggle for independence. It seems he is just looking for a spot in the shade to fix his power sander. Still, I am not going to waste the opportunity.

"Apa anda tahu dia?" (Did you know him?)

"Ya, semua orang tahu Theys Eluay." (Yes, everyone knew Theys Eluay.)

"Can you tell me about him?"

"He was a nice man. He made a lot of speeches. He tried to get us our freedom."

I ask a few follow up questions and he gives me short, unengaged answers. He goes back to fixing his power sander. When he finishes, he looks up at me, "Do you want to go to his house?"

We walk just a couple blocks down a side street to a building that looks more like a community center than a house. It is the headquarters of *Satgas Papua* (Papua Task Force) and the home of Theys Eluay's son, Boy Eluay. A spiritual teacher and one of Boy Eluay's advisors invite me to meet the man they refer to as "The Leader." As I sit waiting for them to walk me over, a couple jolly locals try to sell me a hat made from exotic and endangered Bird of Paradise feathers.

Four of Boy Eluay's advisors, all neatly dressed, are sitting with him on a shaded patio. Boy Eluay, who is much younger, wears camouflage cargo shorts, a baseball cap and black t-shirt covering his overweight body. He looks up at me with glossy eyes and remains seated as he shakes my hand. While I always try not to judge a book by its cover, I can not help but think that Boy Eluay looks and carries himself more like a guy who is the head of an East Los Angeles gang than a freedom movement.

I tell the men about my trip across Indonesia. They are only interested in what I think of Papua. They tell me that the U.S. must help Papua gain independence. Amos, one of the advisors says, "Your president lived in Indonesia. Now he must live in Papua!"

Boy Eluay grants me permission to interview him. I ask my questions in English and Indonesian and where my Indonesian is a little off, Amos repeats the question more clearly for me.

"What is the mission of *Satgas Papua?*"

"We are the security of Papua. We want to bring freedom to Papua."

"What is your short-term objective right now?"

"To open up a dialogue with Indonesia. We do not want trouble. We do not want to kill. But Indonesia will not even give us a dialogue."

"What are some of the ways Papuans are discriminated against?" Boy looks to his advisors to take this question, and one does, "Our schools are not free to teach as they please. We have a unique history. Why does Indonesia send the same textbooks to Papua that they send to Sumatra?"

"Why did the Indonesian military kill your father?"

Boy Eluay stares at me for a few seconds without blinking, *"Karena mereka bisa."* (Because they could.)

I ask Boy Eluay about the recent violence in Papua. One of his advisors quickly ends my short interview. He suggests I email him my questions, and he would be happy to record Boy's responses and email right back.

My emails would all go ignored. I later learned that locals' opinion of Boy Eluay ranges from, "We as Papuans were behind his father, Theys Eluay. Only some of us support Boy Eluay," to, "He is a fat womanizer and a drunk." An International Relations graduate student seemed embarrassed that foreigners would accept Boy Eluay as the leader of their struggle.

After reaching the main road and walking just a half block, I see a yellow Mitsubishi dump truck screeching to a halt. Even though we did not plan to meet for another hour, Diang looks frustrated and is yelling at me. He says he was worried about me and has been driving all around town looking for me. Shots were fired from the mountains. Diang did not know if anyone was killed, but there were surely serious injuries. He says that all workers were told to go home immediately. I hop in and apologize for troubling him. We are both quiet for most of the ride. For the last few miles, Diang's mix tape is rolling, and I resume my job of translating, "*Sungai sepi mendesah, Menunggu untuk aku. Menunggu untuk aku.*" (Lonely rivers sigh, Wait for me. Wait for me.)

***

Sarah gives me great news early on my second to last full day in Papua. The military has opened up the road to the border again, and she has called a driver to take us. The trip will be about two-and-a-half hours each way. My sole reason for dragging Sarah on a five hour car ride is so that I can officially complete my trip that started three thousand two hundred some odd miles and many stories ago at Kilometer Zero in Aceh.

The road is smoothly paved leading straight east. We pass through a few villages and at times the Pacific is all we can see to our left. Most of the ride slices through bushy trees with the Papuan jungle hiding behind mountains to our right. On one stretch of road, Sarah casually says, "This is where they kill people." I look over at her and she adds, "But, don't worry. Today it is safe."

An occasional motorbike passes us on the otherwise still road. In the last village before the border we slow down to drive around a group of girls walking to school together in their uniform red dresses and white shirts. One girl, maybe seven years old, pumps her fist in the air and shouts, "*Merdeka!*"

About a half hour from the border we turn with a bend in the road and see a few stalls of old women selling fruit and vegetables. On the other side of the road in the distance there is a parked pick-up truck. It is the only other passenger vehicle we have seen in over an hour. We are cruising by at about 35 miles an hour. As the truck comes into view I can see there are a lot of people standing on the back flatbed. Once I am able to make out who they are, I take a deep breath and my heart stops.

They are a tribe of Papuans from the jungle wearing their traditional dress, which is almost nothing, and holding bow and arrows. They stare into the backseat at me as we drive by. Sarah points, "Look jungle people. Don't take picture." The only time I ever felt anything like I felt at that moment was when I entered Yellowstone National Park and saw a bison on the road creeping toward my car.

As the "jungle people" get smaller and less threatening through the back window, I ask the driver to stop. I try to gauge Sarah to see how foolish it would be to go back and talk to them.

"If you want to talk to them go talk."

I get out of the car and walk back. I stop at one of the fruit stalls to buy an apple, ease my nerves and rehearse a few questions in Indonesian. I look both ways before crossing the street. There is not another car anywhere near us. The sun is scorching down even harder than usual, and I am sweating before I even say a word.

"Selamat Pagi! Aku Kevin dari Amerika. Aku menulis buku tentang. . ." (Good Morning! I am Kevin from America. I am writing a book about. . .) I continue with a long, jittery speech on why I am here, how much I love Papua and am interested in learning more about her people.

About fifteen men with bodies and faces painted with mud and five women, who I am sure are not use to covering their chests, stare at me with no discernible reaction. I look across the street and see Sarah at the fruit stall. I wave her over. As she approaches I am nervously explaining how Sarah and I became friends, "*Ini website nama Couch Surfing.*" Sarah motions for me to shut up, "They don't understand *Bahasa* Indonesian!"

Of course. They have lived in the jungle their entire lives. They hunt their own food and are some of the last truly nomadic people left on this earth in 2011. They never attended an Indonesian school. The island of New Guinea contains over one thousand indigenous languages, one out of every six in the world. These people have their own language that most likely only a few hundred people can speak.

Sarah starts speaking, and after awhile one of the men responds to her. She looks over at me, "I have spent a lot of time in the jungle. I remember a few words that most jungle people can understand. They trust me because they can tell by my scent that I have lived in the jungle." I look over at these stern faces and wide noses and wonder what they can tell by my scent.

Sarah tries to translate a few of my questions, but we do not get very far. I do learn that they have traded food to rent this pick-up truck, and they are on their way to downtown Jayapura, where they plan to protest tomorrow. I wish them luck.

Back on the other side of the street, I stare across at these people that are from as different a culture as any human beings I have ever met. I look at their bow and arrows. I bet they have a lot more experience shooting those than they do exercising their right to protest. I ask Sarah why they would bring weapons to a protest. "The cops and soldiers have their guns so they have their bow and arrows." The statement makes perfect sense, but only if I think about it without taking into account the power structure of the world.

We walk back to the car and drive the last few miles to the border, which ends up being just as unremarkable as Sarah predicted it would be. We find a cousin of Sarah's working there, and she cooks us a free *mie goreng* (fried noodles) meal. I spend the entire following day walking around downtown Jayapura asking if anyone knows anything about a protest or if anyone has seen a truckload of Papuans from the jungle. No one knows anything, and the story of the people in that pick-up truck takes its place with the rest of my Indonesian stories, with endings I will never know.

***

My last morning in Papua I awake to the sound of intense yelling reverberating through Sarah's apartment. Everyone is speaking a Papuan language so I can not understand a word. There is some kind of scuffle happening in the apartment unit adjoined to Sarah's place. There is just a thin wall separating my sleeping mat from the noise next door. When the wall begins to shudder I realize that it has turned physical. Sarah walks out of her room. She warns me to stay inside. When she returns she tells me that her neighbor is in charge of finding tenants to fill a new housing unit on the new side of town. Many families have already paid him the deposit, and they should have been able to move in weeks ago. Now they are afraid that it is all a scam, and each one wants to personally make this man understand what will happen to him if they do not either move in or get their money back soon.

I peek out the window. There are about twenty Papuan men, most with their shirts off, showing off their brawny chests and waiting their turn to enter the house and throw this amateur real estate tycoon around. At one point Sarah yells at the angry men and tells them to go home and stop acting like little boys. They yell at her to mind her own business. Sitting on my sleeping mat I listen to the systematic commotion. Each time two men walk into the house. The conversation starts off civil enough. Then the pace and volume of the tenants' voices pick up. There are a few words of rebuttal from the neighboring landlord, and as if right on cue, the landlord is tossed repeatedly against the wall, causing an uproar that drowns out the female shrieks for mercy. Eventually the wall banging stops, a departing threat or two are hurled, and the men leave. Then our neighbor waits with his door open for the next pair of men to walk in and for the entire process to repeat itself. It is the most orderly act of mayhem I have ever experienced.

The scene it is a testament to how Papuans have and still handle conflict. This fact that Papuans never created city centers with checks and balances to keep order, but instead roamed their land in clans hunting and gathering food speaks of the importance in Papuan society of being able to solve their own issues. Papuans, like all groups of people before the creations of police departments and court rooms, took on the responsibility of handling disputes among themselves. Having a non-confrontational personality was not an option. When there was a problem you had to face the person directly.

The inherent fuel to shed blood when deemed necessary has not emptied from the spirit of Papuans. In *An Empire of the East*, published in 1993, Norman Lewis describes a mock battle that took place between members of Papua's Yali tribe. Unemployed men were hired to dress up as warriors and wave spears and shoot arrows for the enjoyment of spectators. One guy must have had trouble holding back his aggression, which spread like wildfire, and the show ended with a death toll of sixteen.[29]

Now I can easily relate because I have had a number of spontaneous wrestling matches with childhood and college buddies that ended with pretty nasty rug burns and hard feelings all around, but I still can not imagine taking part in an activity that starts out as horseplay and ends with sixteen bodies being carried off.

After breakfast the mob of angry men are gone. When I go outside, also gone is my only pair of leather sandals. I look all around the front porch and realize that one of the men must have found them too good to pass up. I want to handle the situation like a local would, but I have no idea how to find the guy I am supposed to repeatedly throw against a wall. Instead I walk back inside barefoot and whine to Sarah's aunt.

By some stroke of luck Sarah has put together a gift package for me, and the first item she pulls out of the bag is a pair of black flip-flops. If I was in any other part of the country, it would be near impossible to find a size-13 sandal, but fortunately Papua has plenty of big feet. The rest of my goodie bag includes a Papuan t-shirt, a sleeveless jersey with a hood, a box of sardines, a hand-made bag, a leather wallet and a *koteka* (penis gourd), just in case I want to go with a funkier look my next time in a club.

After our good-byes it is time for me to board my ship. The same setup as last time, long rows of sleeping spaces, not much wider than an ironing board. Only this time every sleeping space is already taken, largely thanks to the gang of Papuan men who muscle their way past security and claim spaces for those passengers smart enough to pay them. After a couple laps around the ship I start searching for the best available floor space. Even the good floor spaces away from busy footpaths are taken. I see a spot along the stairwell, and I drop my backpack. It is better than sleeping on the outside deck. Before I begin to construct a bed with my clothes, two gracious families, one Papuan, one Ambonese, call me over to join them. I toss my backpack on top of theirs. They clear a small space for me where I will sleep for the next three nights. If I were to flail my arms and legs I would hit at least eight people.

"There's nothing nobler than to put up with a few inconveniences likes snakes and dust for the sake of absolute freedom." – Jack Kerouac.

As we set sail I walk out to the port side deck of the ship. The Pacific is a metallic, navy blue that is swallowing the last rays of sunlight, rays that will soon create an autumn sunrise in New York. By Thanksgiving I will be there, sleeping in a bed, speaking only English, sitting on toilet seats, and not eating rice.

The green mountains have transformed to a black silhouette. I realize I never even penetrated more than a couple miles from the coast. Of every place I have passed through, Papua is the biggest mystery and the place I crave most to see again.

Ship from Ambon *ke* Papua

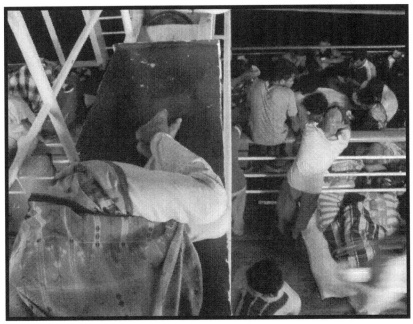

Ship from Ambon *ke* Papua

Conclusion

I spent some time in Padang before flying home. After selling my pearls from Aceh to Papua, bargaining endless hours, watching at least a hundred Indonesian women walk off wearing my jewelry and about another fifty men, including plenty of cops and soldiers, with gifts in hand, my luck came to an end. I was selling at the beach when I got pinched by three plain clothes cops. One demanded I get on the back of his motorbike and take a ride to the station. After a lot of arguing, I drove myself to the station, but not before calling a few friends to make sure they knew where I was.

I sat on a couch in a fairly comfortable room for three hours with Padang's Good Cop, Bad Cop and Silent Cop. They drilled me with questions ranging from my travels to my love life. Most I did not bother answering and just asked them to tell me what it was going to cost me. The Bad Cop kept accusing me of being an American spy, "Maybe you are intelligence. Maybe I am intelligence. How can we know?" I was fairly sure that no one would categorize any of them, or myself for that matter, as intelligence.

They pulled out my entire collection of jewelry one piece at a time and asked how much each item was worth. I assumed that would be the last time I saw the pearls and stones, and just wanted to pay the inevitable bribe and get out of there.

Then I decided to take my chances and pull every card I had. "You know I am a good friend of the Prince of Ternate." None of the cops looked impressed. They waited for me to pull the next card.

"I was a professor for one year at Andalas University." They nodded, looking somewhat impressed, but it was not going to save me.

"I have a close friend in Indonesia's KPK (Indonesian acronym for Anti-Corruption Agency)." Good Cop's eyebrows rose, but after a short discussion in their local Minang language, I could see that I had not instilled any fear in them.

And then my last card dropped. "I am writing a book about Indonesia. . . Yes, that is why I have all these books and notebooks in my bag." I could tell I had their attention, and that I better make my finish strong. I started recalling the introduction to this book.

"This book is going to take all the dramatic history, current events and social issues of this 17,000 island archipelago and tell it through the raw lens of my journey from the western shores of Sumatra to the jungles of Papua. . . The book will paint a picture of Indonesia in 2011, how it was born and the direction it is headed in. The story will grow from interactions with the Indonesian people, particularly how they treat foreigners (long pause), as well as what they want out of life and the obstacles and opportunities in front of them. It will be a mosaic. Muslim-Christian relations will improve. Any of you guys ever read *On The Road?*"

The three cops looked confused and uneasy. "Did I mention I have a big publisher awaiting my manuscript in New York? And within months it will be read by thousands of Americans."

Bad Cop and Silent Cop left the room to speak with the captain. I sat with Good Cop and watched the History Channel.

The two cops returned with their captain. Bad Cop spoke up, "You know that we have the power to confiscate your jewelry, deport you and fine you thousands of U.S. dollars? Instead our captain has decided to let your actions slide this one time since you are a foreigner and probably did not know any better." Quiet cop elbowed me to start thanking the captain.

After a half hour of "Makasihs" and telling them what an amazing place Indonesia is and how I can not wait to write about it, the five of us moved to an outdoor café where the captain told anyone who would listen that he could have confiscated my jewelry, deported me and fined me thousands of U.S. dollars, but (this is when they would look at me to finish the story) instead out of the goodness of their hearts and the reverence they have for their positions, they are letting me off scot-free.

***

Before I knew it my trip was over and I was *pulang* (to return home), sitting in a bus bound for the airport in standstill Jakarta traffic. I was ready to get home, but not quite ready to leave Indonesia. I recalled a feeling I had at different points of the trip, when I was on a ferry crossing from Java to Bali, when I was taking in the music of Padang's *Pasar Seni*, when I was driving a motorbike around the enchanted late night streets of Jogja, when I was on the outdoor deck of that ship reading and hearing stories about Papua. It was a feeling as fleeting as a wave and as powerful as anything I have ever experienced.

I felt that I could just spend the rest of my life crisscrossing those islands, selling things out of my backpack, allowing myself to be showered by the kindness of strangers, noting the changes, tasting the spices, listening to the stories about who these people are and sharing them on neighboring islands to the neighbors they never met.

What would change? What would stay the same? Would moral police still harass Karina's neighborhood and other young, kissing couples across Indonesia's beaches? Would the Papuans and Acehnese ever fully integrate into Indonesia, or would an all out war come first? Would the neighborhoods in Ambon desegregate and would the faces in that city ever soften? Has *Anak Krakatau* inherited her mother's temper, and will she blow her lid in my lifetime? Would there always be kind souls like Venus to brighten up a traveler's birthday? Will this country ever recognize that one of the greatest writers that ever lived is of their own blood and honor him by reading his books?

But then I thought even if I did spend the rest of my life here, how could I ever possibly understand Indonesia? Indonesia does not even understand itself. There is still a childish innocence to Indonesia, a state of not knowing what it will look like when it grows into its body, its acne clears up and it has to choose its role in the world.

It is not fair to personify Indonesia into one person. No, Indonesia is more like a big dysfunctional American family where hormone-crazy daughters rebel against every rule their parents hand down, and a couple weird sons want to make those rules stricter. Where grumpy old people bicker about the grandsons marrying minorities, and every marriage could break at any second. Aunts that refuse to speak to each other, in-laws who were never given a chance to explain themselves so most just accept someone else's version, screaming babies that do not get enough attention. And then there are the non-human problems, like the puppy who just when things are looking calm will chew up the couch pillows and crap on everyone's bed. But somehow they still make up one family, and every holiday they show up under the same roof to celebrate and brawl.

There was so much I wanted to understand and experience. There were pirates I never met hiding on tiny swampy islands off Sumatra, holding up ships and ransoming them for millions of dollars. There was so much more jungle and wildlife, the largest plant in the world, environmentalists waging war against pollution and deforestation, more surviving hunter-gatherer cultures in the Mentawai Islands and the illustrious women of North Sulawesi. I could see that Indonesia had become an even bigger mystery to me than it was when I first stepped foot on it almost four years ago.

Then I tried to concentrate on what I did see. My mind flew on a bird's back over the long map of Indonesia, watching what was happening in each part of it right that second. I peeked in to the coffee shops in Aceh to see Norman and Hijrah talking up some young girls about Mecca, skirted through West Sumatra, where old Bactair Naik was planting his crops and still bragging about the CIA spy that thanked him for his service. I peeked through a Surabaya loft filled with girls from Kalimantan and Sumatra and guys from Java and Flores and questioned if they ever wonder about their own great grandparents, how none of them could have communicated with each other or had even heard of the word Indonesia. I watched the annoying hawkers in Bali waking up Kuta, and of course I saw Azhar's giant frame walking along Ambon's Bay to the Tulehu Mosque.

Did I write about them the best I could? I wrote so much about war, revolutions and future threats of violence. But in all my time in Indonesia, I never felt threatened or witnessed someone strike another person in anger. With the exception of a few immigration offices, I was treated like a prince, actually much better than a prince, from one side of the country to the other.

Before I let myself get washed away with thoughts of what the trip and the book could have been, I was comforted, as I have been many times, by remembering the fitting words of a writer;

"Do not judge the trifling of man with your simple eyes;

Even if your sight was as acute as a hawk's,

your mind as sharp as a razor,

your touch more sensitive than a god,

even if your ears could grasp music and the wailing lament of life,

your knowledge of mankind

will never be close to complete."

-Pramoedya Anata Toer

The last person I thought about was Gusti, the starry-eyed, young soul from South Sumatra setting out on his first journey alone. I had tried to contact him by phone and email, but with no success.

Months ago he had sat next to me on a much rustier bus that never made a complete stop for him, on his way to take his first job. There was a good chance he was somewhere in that same ocean of a Jakarta traffic jam, driving an important businessman to the airport. The businessman would be sitting in the back, reading today's Jakarta Globe, smoking a cigarette. Gusti would be at the wheel, still baby-faced, trying to find a radio station he thought the businessman would like, probably smoking himself by now. Unless some extraordinary stroke of luck strikes Gusti, his eyes will never see what I have seen in the course of my trip. Not the whipping ceremony in Ambon or Borobudur Temple. Not the destruction of the Boxing Day tsunami or Malin Kundang's stone. He will never be overcome by the vitality of his land or marvel at the differing attributes of the people that make up his country. He will not shake hands with any rebel leaders, vice-mayors or even a Papuan. And the suit in his back seat, who can easily afford to take my trip without having to sell or barter pearls and stones along the way, will never see the point in it all.

I wonder who will ever see the point in it all.

Acknowledgements

For everything and more, Thank You Mom and Dad.

For their diligent work editing this book, Thank you Gloria Hatrick, Laura Di Fabio, Corynn Robinson, Joshua Beard, Tegnan Hilaire. Thank you for feedback from Andrew Bailey, Christopher Byck, Bryan Close and Desmon Nusantara.

Thank you to those who helped me get to Indonesia or gave me the push I needed to write this book, C, Amy, Luis, Bryan, Ed, J Beard, Hawkes, Marcos, Daronzio, Darren, Ram, Tehya, Santo, Verito.

For giving me a home in Padang, Tegnan, Mamad, Da Jon, Desmon, Novel, Erlangga, Bayoe, everyone at *Pasar Seni*, Belanak and *Mak Etak, Terima Kasih.*

For my literary inspiration in writing this book, Thank you Rob Gifford, James Frey, Arthur Nersesian, JR Moeringer, Peter Hessler, Jon Krakauer, Dorothy Bryant, Erick Setiawan and Pram.

For helping me get from Aceh to Papua, Thank you Bhayu, Jenny, Richard, and everyone at Andalas. Thank you Norman, Hijrah, Didi (The Three Idiots), Annie, Charlie, Fernando. Thank you Harpa, Alberto, Ita, Lia, Venus. Thank you *Ibu* Syahmainar, Denny, Fahir, everyone from *Nusa Indah.* Thank you Fani, Romi, Putri, Fifi, Minggus, Haniel, Diang. Thank you

Karina. Thank you Winda, P-jaks, everyone from the Surabaya flat and *Taman Bukul*. Thank you *Pak* Sus, *Mas* Butet, Derry Brian, Sole. Thank you Azhar. Thank you *Ibu* Ga and your family in Tulehu. Thank you Mama Joe, *Pak* Robert, Prelly, Riki, and your family. Thank you Benny, Grace and all of your family in Makassar. Thank you Ben, Ishita, Greg, Lucy, Jimmy, Tuvu, Silvy, Claudia. Thank you Joan.

Thank you to those who prepared me for this, friends from Bregano, Marymount, Suzhou, Notre Dame, especially my crew in Yonkers.

Thank God for my big, loving Irish family and Thank you to everyone in it.

To anyone who ever listened to me mumble and gave me the confidence and insanity to dedicate so much to this book, Thank you.

Indonesian – English Glossary

Anak – child

Anggur – wine

Bagus – good

Bahasa – language

Becak – a bicycle rickshaw with the passenger seat in front.

Biasa – usual

Bintang – star, name of most common national beer

Bohong – lie

Bu (short for Ibu) – mother, title given to a much older woman

Bukit – hill

Bule – white person, foreigner

Buku – book

Cantik – beautiful (mostly used regarding people)

Da – title given to a man slightly older in Minang culture

Dia – he, she

Dukun – shaman, spiritual healer

Idul Fitri – the most important Muslim holiday, marking the end of Ramadan.

Indah – beautiful (regarding scenery)

Ikan Bakar – burnt fish

Jalan – street

Jalan-Jalan – taking a walk/ out and about/ most common response to "*Mau ke mana?*"

Jilbab – headscarf

Kantor Imigrasi – Immigration Office

Ke – to

Kopi – coffee

Kreteks – hand-wrapped, clove flavored cigarettes

Lubang Buaja – Crocodile Hole

Macet – traffic

Makan – *food*

Makan pagi – breakfast (literally: morning food)

Makasih – thanks

Marga – Batak family line

Mau – want

Mau ke mana? – Where are you going? (common greeting)

Menunggu – to wait

Merdeka – independence, freedom

Mie Goreng – fried noodles

Merantau – Cultural tradition in West Sumatra that a young man leave his hometown to make a better life for himself

Nama – name

Nasi – rice

Nasi Goreng – fried rice

Nusa – type of flower

Nyamuk – mosquito

Ojek – motorbike that acts as a taxi

Pak (short for Bapak) – father, title given to much older men, Sir

Pantai – beach

Pasar – market

Pulau – island

Pulang – to return home

Rendang – beef and fried rice mixed with spices and a brown coconut milk sauce

Rujuck – a mix of tropical fruits covered in a dark spicy peanut sauce

Rumah Makan – restaurant

Sate – strips of meat eaten on skewers

Saya – I, me

Sehat – healthy

Selamat Pagi – Good Morning

Selimut – blanket

Sendiri – alone

Seni – art

Sudah – done, finished, already (common response to *"Sudah makan?")*

Sudah makan – Have you eaten? (common greeting)

Susu – milk

Tantara – army

Terima Kasih – thank you

Timor – East, an island of Indonesia

Toko – store

Endnotes

[1] Andrew Vltchek & Rossie Indira, *Exile: Conversations with Pramoedya Ananta Toer* (Chicago: Haymarket Books, 2006) p 153.

[2] Graham Saunders, *Customs and Etiquette of Indonesia (*London: Kuperard Publishers & Distributors, 2007).

[3] Pramoedya Ananta Toer, *Footsteps* (New York: Penguin Books; Reprint edition, 1996) p 66.

[4] Pramoedya Ananta Toer, *Footsteps* (New York: Penguin Books; Reprint edition, 1996) p 67.

[5] K'tut Tantri, *Revolt in Paradise: One Woman's Fight for Freedom in Indonesia* (Potter Style; Reprint edition, 1989) p 164.

[6] *Indonesia: Djago, the Rooster*. Time Magazine. March 10, 1958 (Accessed October 18, 2016). http://content.time.com/time/subscriber/article/0,33009,863059,00.html

[7] James DiEugenio, Lisa Pease & Judge Joe Brown. "JFK, Indonesia, CIA & Freeport Sulphur." Real History Archives. (Accessed October 19, 2016). http://www.realhistoryarchives.com/collections/hidden/freeport-indonesia.htm

[8] Dierdre Griswold. *The Second Greatest Crime of the Century: 1958: The First CIA Attempt.* Worker's World. 1998. (Accessed October 18, 2016). http://www.workers.org/indonesia/chap2.html

[9] Baskara T. Wardaya, *Cold War Shadow: United States Policy Toward Indonesia, 1953-1963*, (Yokyakarta: PUSdEP - Pusat Sejarah dan Etika Politik/Center for History and Political Ethics in collaboration with Galangpress, 2007) p 244.

[10] Baskara T. Wardaya, *Cold War Shadow: United States Policy Toward Indonesia, 1953-1963*, (Yokyakarta: PUSdEP - Pusat Sejarah dan Etika Politik/Center for History and Political Ethics in collaboration with Galangpress, 2007) p 193.

[11] Baskara T. Wardaya, *Cold War Shadow: United States Policy Toward Indonesia, 1953-1963*, (Yokyakarta: PUSdEP - Pusat Sejarah dan Etika Politik/Center for History and Political Ethics in collaboration with Galangpress, 2007) p 244.

[12] Barack Obama, *Dreams from my Father: A Story of Race and Inheritance*, (New York: Broadway Books, 2004).

[13] David Maraniss, *Barack Obama: The Story* (New York: Simon & Schuster; Reprint edition, 2013) p 225.

[14] Joseph Conrad, *Lord Jim* (London: Penguin Books, 2007, Originally Published by Blackwood's Magazine, 1900).

[15] Tineke Hellwig (editor) and Eric Tagliacozzo (editor), *The Indonesian Reader: History, Culture, Politics (The World Readers)* (Durham, North Carolina: Duke University Press Books, 2009) chapter VIII.

[16] Lloyd Parry, *In the Time of Madness: Indonesia on the Edge of Chaos* (New York: Grove Press, 2007) p 90.

[17] Stefan Eklof, *Indonesia Politics in Crisis: The Long Fall of Suharto, 1996-1998* (Copenhagen: Nordic Institute of Danish Studies, 2002).

[18] John Steinbeck, *Travels with Charley* (New York: Viking Press, 1962) p 58.

[19] VS Naipul, *Among the Believers: An Islamic Journey* (New York: Vintage; Reissue Edition 1982) p 358.

[20] Timothy Lindsay, *The Romance of K'tut Tantri and Indonesia* (London: Equinox Publishing, 2008) p 8.

[21] William Blum. "War and Pornography." Third World Traveller. (Excerpt from *Killing Hope*). (Accessed October 18, 2016). http://www.thirdworldtraveler.com/Blum/Indonesia57_KH.html

[22] "Manipulated Message Causes Clash in Indonesia." VIVAnews. (Accessed September 1, 2011). http://en.vivanews.com/news/read/246268-manipulated-message-causes-clash-in-indonesia

[23] Jared Diamond, *Guns, Germs and Steel: The Fates of Human Societies* (New York: W. W. Norton & Company, 1999) p 298.

[24] Karishma Vaswani. "US Firm Struggles to Escape Its Past in Papua." BBC News. August 8, 2011. (Accessed October 18, 2016). http://www.bbc.com/news/world-asia-pacific-14417718

[25] Aubrey Belford. "Thousands Rally to Press for Independence from Indonesia." New York Times. August 2, 2011. (Accessed October 18, 2016). http://www.nytimes.com/2011/08/03/world/asia/03indonesia.html?_r=0

[26] "Machete Attack Kills Four in Indonesia's Papua." Trend News Agency. August 1, 2011. (Accessed October 18, 2016). http://en.trend.az/world/other/1912695.html

[27] Charles E. Farhadian and Stephan Babuljak, *The Testimony Project: Papua: A Collectioin of Personal Histories in West Papua* (West Papua: Penerbit Deiyai, 2007) p 78.

[28] Charles E. Farhadian and Stephan Babuljak, *The Testimony Project: Papua: A Collectioin of Personal Histories in West Papua* (West Papua: Penerbit Deiyai, 2007) p 30.

[29] Norman Lewis, *An Empire of the East*, (London: Eland Books, 1993).

Other References

John H. McGlynn (editor), *Indonesia in the Soeharto Years: Issues, Incidents and Images* (Jakarta: Lontar/KITLV, 2007).

Michael Vatikiotis, *The Spice Garden* (London: Equinox Publishing, 2003).

Simon Winchester, *Krakatoa: The Day the World Exploded* (London: Harper Perennial, 2005).

About the Author

Kevin Lee first visited Indonesia in 2008. After teaching at Andalas University in West Sumatra, he journeyed the length of the country in 2011, a trip this book is based on. He studied Political Science at Marymount University in Virginia and holds a Master's in Education from the University of Notre Dame. *Leaving Indonesia* is his first book.

Kevin grew up in Yonkers, New York and now lives in Brooklyn. He is self-employed. On weekends from St. Patty's Day through Christmas, Kevin sells his pearls on 39 Prince Street in Manhattan at the NoLita Outdoor Artisan Market. He can be reached at kevinleeindo@gmail.com

Made in the USA
Middletown, DE
27 December 2016